Kuala Lumpur

Front cover: the bright lights of one
of the Petronas Twin Towers

Right: elegant colonial architecture

TOP 10 ATTRACTIONS

Kuala Gandah National Elephant Conservation Centre • A chance to observe, ride and feed Asian elephants *(page 79)*

Colonial core • Majestic Mughal-style architecture of the late 19th century *(page 26)*

Nightspots • From sophisticated bars to hot clubs, KL offers great nightlife options *(page 87)*

Batu Caves • A beautiful limestone cave temple with Hindu shrines and statues *(page 75)*

Central Market • Home to lively art and craft shops *(page 31)*

Sin Sze Si Ya Temple • An important Taoist temple that honours city founder Yap Ah Loy *(page 32)*

Rumah Penghulu Abu Seman • A rare ancient Malay timber house in modern KL *(page 72)*

Islamic Arts Museum • Artefacts from the Muslim world displayed in a graceful building *(page 53)*

Canopy Walkway • Walk among the treetops at the Forest Research Institute of Malaysia *(page 77)*

Petronas Twin Towers • These skyscrapers, among the world's tallest, are stunning both day and night *(page 58)*

58

11

97

CONTENTS

Features

69

60

26

INTRODUCTION

Kuala Lumpur – or KL, as it is fondly called – is proudly progressive and cosmopolitan, aspiring to achieve 'world-class city' status by 2020. The trademarks of this ambition include an ever-changing skyscraper skyline, the conspicuous presence of global brand names and an educated populace as well-versed in English Premier League politics as China's superpower potential. However, visitors to KL are likely to be impressed most with its multi-ethnic Asian rhythms, colour and bustle. From myriad cultural and religious sites and festivals, to a mouth-wateringly large choice of food, the multifaceted threads of Malay, Chinese, Indian and other Asian traditions and sensibilities are intricately woven into the fabric of this city.

A Capital City

Kuala Lumpur is the capital of Malaysia, which comprises Peninsular Malaysia and the states of Sabah and Sarawak on the island of Borneo. Located midway down the peninsula's west coast, KL has an area of 234 sq km (90 sq miles). It anchors Klang Valley, the country's most developed and prosperous conurbation, which spreads over 1,600 sq km (618 sq miles) and has a population of 4.5 million, over half of whom work in KL. Annexed from the state of Selangor, KL is one of the country's three Federal Territories and the seat of Parliament. The administrative and judicial capital is Putrajaya in the south.

Like the rest of Malaysia, KL is hot, sunny and humid all year round. The temperature is highest between 11am–1pm, when it is a good idea to spend time indoors at any of the air-

The spectacular Petronas Twin Towers by night

conditioned attractions. The city's oldest sections date back 150 years, but much of the city was modernised in the 1990s, when the country experienced double-digit Gross Domestic Product growth, fuelling a property and infrastructure boom. Many old neighbourhoods have been redeveloped, and post-modern architecture dominates the cityscape. Big city problems like pollution, traffic and high crime rates have taken root. Nonetheless, visitors are often surprised at how green KL is, with parks and gardens within the city and lush rainforests on its outskirts. The latter make up the natural tropical forests that cover about 40 percent of Malaysia; these are among the most species-rich in the world.

Mopeds on Petaling Street

An Economic Magnet

The indigenous Orang Asli people are believed to have been the first inhabitants of the area, but they have long been relegated to the city's fringes. Many of today's KL-ites actually have their roots elsewhere in the country. The current generation relocated to KL in the 1960s, when the country's economy shifted from an agricultural to industrial base. They were drawn by jobs and good facilities, and now enjoy the country's highest per capita GDP and best employment rates. This is why KL continues to attract youngsters from all over Malaysia, as well as migrant workers from other countries, upon whom the city's economy heavily relies.

The 1960s generation of KL-ites retain strong ties to their home towns. At no time is this more strongly manifested than during the major festivals of Chinese New Year and Hari Raya Puasa, when the city empties out

> **Malaysian English**
>
> KL-ites use a wide variety of English, from east coast American to Received Pronunciation, and versions infused with vocabulary from any or all of the local languages. What is evident is that KL-ites love their English and have fun with it.

during the *balik kampung* ('going home') exodus. Increasingly, though, these homeland ties are being broken as their children become more urbanised, affluent, internet-dependent and connected to the world beyond Malaysia.

Multiple Cultures

Ethnically, KL's 2 million inhabitants are made up of a majority of Chinese and Malays and a minority of Indians. However, these simplistic categories cannot encapsulate the rainbow of peoples that make up a social landscape that goes back to the beginning of trade in the Malay peninsula in AD200. Over the centuries, assimilations and adaptations have been motley, creative and widespread in everything from language to architecture, fashion to social mores. The contemporary influences of education, affluence and globalisation continue to iron out ethnic differences.

Nonetheless, core ethnic values are retained, especially when it comes to religion. The Chinese are largely Buddhists/ Taoists or Christian, the Malays are Muslim *(see box, page 10)* and the Indians Hindu, Muslim or Christian. Other faiths practised include Sikhism and Bahai. Constitutionally, Islam is the official religion, but what this means is currently being debated because there are two parallel justice systems, one for Muslims, the other for non-Muslims. Recent high-profile cases involving conversion of one spouse to Islam has brought this dichotomy into the limelight. Nonetheless, freedom of religion is generally guaranteed, as is evident in the coexistence of different places of worship and religious celebrations throughout the city.

Tourist-friendly

As the country's financial and commercial centre, Kuala Lumpur has a large number of global service centres for accountancy, advertising, banking and law. The city is leading national efforts towards developing a services-based economy, one of the city's key income-earners being tourism. As such, KL is tourist-oriented, offering among other things easily available tourist information and clear signposts to key attractions.

The Malays

Originally from southern China and Taiwan, Malays (the *Melayu* people) arrived in the Malay archipelago 3,000–5,000 years ago. Through the years, they intermarried and assimilated with other Chinese, Indians, Arabs and Thais. Malaysia's Federal Constitution defines a Malay as one who practises Islam and Malay culture, speaks the Malay language, and whose ancestors are Malays. To renounce Islam is considered apostasy. Malay culture shows strong Javanese, Sumatran, Siamese and especially Indian influence. Linguistically, Malay is Austronesian, but people will recognise vocabulary that is Arabic, Sanskrit, Tamil, Portuguese, Dutch, Chinese and English.

Malays are also grouped officially as *bumiputra*, literally 'sons of the soil'. This political term was coined to ensure Malays' constitutional 'special position', the basis for indigenity and hence affirmative rights. *Bumiputra* also encompasses the indigenous people of the peninsula, Sabah and Sarawak, as well as Indian Muslims and Thai and Portuguese Malaysians.

The city was also recently spruced up for Visit Malaysia Year 2007. The hospitality industry is well organised and largely English-speaking. However, service standards might not be up to par in some hotels and restaurants, particularly with the growing dependence on migrant workers whom local bosses have not trained properly.

As KL grew, roughly following the same lines as its colonial period layout, city-planners neglected to make it pedestrian- or disabled-friendly. A saving grace is the existence of good rail systems, which are the only way to get around during the

Musicians in traditional costume

badly gridlocked 8–9.30am and 5–7pm rush hours. Taxis are plentiful, but their drivers are gaining a nasty reputation for charging exorbitant fees during peak hours and after midnight.

Orientation

Navigating the city is fairly easy with a map. Road signs can sometimes be confusing, but friendly KL-ites are at hand to help with directions. Attractions within the city include a wealth of architecture, historical and cultural enclaves, shopping and dining. There are, in addition, plenty of day-long excursions to the rural surroundings.

The city basically has two centres. The old city centre is at the confluence of the rivers Klang and Gombak, where

The bright lights of busy Bintang Walk

settlers first founded KL. West of the confluence is the colonial core, where 19th-century British rulers built their administrative buildings, a collection of majestic Mughal-styled monuments. Southeast of the confluence is the mainly Chinese enclave around Petaling Street, now the site of the city's liveliest night market. North of the confluence is Masjid India, a mainly Indian Muslim area, and north of that, Kampung Baru, the oldest Malay settlement in KL.

The new city centre, called the Kuala Lumpur City Centre (KLCC), is located northeast of the historic part of town and anchors the commercial and business district known as the Golden Triangle. KLCC is the home to the iconic Petronas Twin Towers, among the tallest buildings in the world. South of this are Bukit Bintang – which packs more shops, hotels and restaurants per square kilometre than anywhere else in the country – and the nightlife magnets of the swanky Asian Heritage Row, Jalan P. Ramlee and Changkat Bukit Bintang.

Outside the city, nature-lovers will enjoy the Forest Research Institute of Malaysia, Kuala Gandah Elephant Conservation Centre and the cool highland retreat of Fraser's Hill. Las Vegas types should head to Genting Highlands for its casino and theme parks.

A BRIEF HISTORY

Lush lowland tropical rainforest originally covered the Malay peninsula, which was peopled first by small numbers of indigenous Orang Asli. When Malays and other peoples started settling in the peninsula, the Orang Asli were pushed inland to where forests still existed. However, they remained key to the sourcing of natural forest products for trade. But when tin was discovered and towns began to spring up, the Orang Asli were marginalised.

The Search for Tin

By the middle of the 19th century the Malay peninsula was an ethnically diverse land of plenty, as well as an international trading centre for tin, spices and other natural resources. Locally, this trade was controlled by Malay sultans such as Selangor's Raja Abdullah. Raja Abdullah was based in the area's capital town of Klang, where he could tax goods and produce that came down the main transport artery of the Klang river. He left the running of the area's tin mines to his Chinese managers, who had access to thousands of indentured labourers escaping poverty in China.

It was in search of tin that, in 1857, at the behest of their Malay royal master, 87 Chinese coolies rowed up the Klang river. When they came to a confluence and the waters became too shallow, they continued inland on foot through swamps and hostile jungle. Luckily, they were rewarded with the discovery of tin. Unluckily, all of them soon died of malaria. However, they did manage to set up a camp at their disembarkation point, the confluence of the Klang and Gombak rivers. They called the place Kuala Lumpur, literally Muddy Estuary. That this would one day be a capital city with global aspirations would have been beyond anyone's imagining then.

Yap Ah Loy Takes Control

Kuala Lumpur became another typical mining town, dominated by Chinese and characterised by wooden shanties, squalor, iniquity and fierce rivalries between secret societies. Activities centred on the eastern river bank of the confluence at Market Square, an area now called Medan Pasar Lama. The rabble was led by community leaders called *Kapitan Cina* (literally Chinese Captain), who were largely ineffectual in imposing order until Yap Ah Loy, the third *Kapitan Cina*, took over in 1868. A feared and respected gang leader who was also a relentless peacekeeper, Yap was police chief, judge, tax collector and property developer as well as a brothel and opium den operator. His tenacity and enterprise were what prevented Kuala Lumpur from disappearing

The Great Trading Past

Thanks to its fortuitous location between two major sea routes and monsoonal wind systems, the Malay peninsula has been at the centre of international trade for thousands of years. The trade centred on the Malay archipelago's rich natural resources, particularly spices, which in the peninsula were harvested by the indigenous Orang Asli, who brought these products to the coasts and exchanged them with the Malays. They in turn traded them with merchants from the rest of the archipelago, India and China, with whom trading links go back to AD200.

By the time the great trading empire of Malacca reached its apex in the 15th century, Chinese, Indians, Persians, Arabs and Malays from the rest of the archipelago (now Indonesia) had forged long-standing business and cultural relationships with the locals and each other, established settlements in the peninsula and brought influences that ranged from religion and language to food.

Control of this trade was what attracted the colonising powers from Portugal, then Holland, and finally Britain from the 15th century onwards.

back into the jungle. During his two-decade tenure, he rebuilt the settlement three times, after the Selangor Civil War, a massive fire and an enormous flood.

It was the Civil War (1867–73) that led to British interference in Selangor and Kuala Lumpur. The British had established themselves in the Straits Settlements of Penang, Malacca and Singapore and controlled the maritime trading routes. However, they left local affairs outside these areas to the sultans. As world demand for tin escalated due to the growth of the canning industry, Selangor's local chieftains became more powerful and started fighting over political authority and taxation. Forming alliances became an integral strategy in their warmongering.

Yap Ah Loy

Raja Abdullah had died, but the faction belonging to his son eventually gained control of Selangor through an ally, Tengku Kudin. Tengku Kudin sought and received the support of Yap Ah Loy, but this was not enough. He also borrowed war funds from merchants in Malacca and Singapore and got armed assistance from British authorities. However, merchants and administrators had started to become concerned about their investments and trade stability in Selangor.

British Rule

In 1876, the British installed a Resident in Selangor to extend to the Malay ruler the 'protection' of the British Empire. The Resident's role was basically to ensure that trade would flour-

Frank Swettenham

ish by imposing British regulations and systems.

By 1880, Selangor's capital had been moved from Klang to Kuala Lumpur. Two years later, under British Resident Frank Swettenham, the modernisation of Kuala Lumpur began, utilising funds mobilised once again by Yap Ah Loy. Finally, the wooden shanties were replaced by brick buildings, laterite roads were built to the mining areas, and a railway line constructed that linked Kuala Lumpur to Klang. A Sanitary Board was also established to provide town council services.

KL was a bustling little town at that time. A Malay and Indian Muslim enclave had sprung up north of the river confluence in an area now called Jalan Masjid India. Many of these early settlers were traders and miners of Sumatran, Bugis, Rawa and Mandailing origins, broadly referred to as Malays. Indian Muslim traders also set up shop here. Their wares were textiles and other products from the Indian subcontinent, items long traded in this land. This area north of the confluence also became the main shopping strip for the British colonials.

The main Chinese communities lived east of the confluence, in the enclave around Jalan Petaling, and comprised Hakka and Cantonese peoples. As KL prospered, they came to dominate business and commerce and make up the majority of the town's population. The European quarter was west of the confluence on the hills overlooking the Lake Gardens.

Most of the buildings were double-storey shophouses, whose owners lived upstairs and ran businesses downstairs. There were also thatched and wooden houses and places of worship, as well as modest government buildings. Along Jalan Ampang, new millionaires began to construct mansions.

A Colonial Capital

In 1896, the British formed the Federated Malay States (FMS) to centralise administration and fast-track economic development. By this time, the peninsula was producing more than half the world's tin. KL became the FMS capital and Swettenham its first Resident-General. The town now had to live up to its new status of colonial capital, as well as inspire the confidence of investors. With this in mind, a new government administrative core was constructed, designed to be suitably imposing yet also reflect the Islamic mores of the land.

Swettenham's residence, now the Carcosa Hotel

The imposing Sultan Abdul Samad Building in 1906

Based on their earlier colonial experiences, British town-planners chose to adapt their version of the Mughal architectural style of North India. The administrative core centred on the monumental Sultan Abdul Samad Building, which remained the heart of KL for well over a century.

Unlike the Chinese, few Malays wanted to relocate to Kuala Lumpur. The British plan was to groom a small, elite group of Malays to participate in local administration. To attract them, the colonials established Kampung Baru (literally New Village), north of the confluence, which today remains almost exclusively Malay. British-educated civil servants from South India were brought to Malaya to fill government positions in the railways, plantations and other clerical services. Labourers were also brought in to build the railways. Government quarters were provided for local civil servants in Brickfields, southeast of the city, where bricks were once manufactured to rebuild early KL. Later, railway-marshalling yards were located on Brickfields's northern side – this is now the city's rail transport hub.

By the turn of the century, another economic product, one introduced by the British, took root in Malaya – rubber. Fuelled by the rubber-tyre boom, thousands of hectares of jungle were converted to plantations, and by 1916 rubber surpassed tin as Malaya's main export. Planters started flooding KL's colonial hang-outs. An influx of indentured labour from India changed the social landscape of Malaya again. The British administered what had become a complex plural society as three crude and ill-defined groups: Malays, Chinese and Indians, each identified with specific economic roles to serve the goal of developing the colonial economy.

When World War II began in 1941, the British were ill-prepared to defend the Malay peninsula and fled, allowing the Japanese an easy takeover. Ruling with an iron fist, the Japanese singled out the Chinese for brutalisation. This gave rise to a local, largely Chinese-based communist movement that engaged the Japanese in guerrilla warfare. At the same time, the Japanese encouraged incipient Malay nationalism, which fed into their military and economic plans for Malaya.

Towards Independence

In 1945, the Japanese surrendered and the British returned to Malaya with a centralised administration plan to recover lost economic ground, but with the aim of paving the way for self-rule. As a signatory to the 1941 Atlantic Charter, the British felt bound to return their colonies to independence. They proposed a united nation with equal rights for all ethnic communities. However, the leaders of a rising brand of Malay nationalistic politics rejected the proposal in favour of a federation recognising the sovereignty of the sultans, the individuality of the states and Malay privileges. At the forefront of

Surrender ceremony

Tunku Abdul Rahman (at the podium) declares independence

this nationalism was the United Malays National Organization (UMNO), the Malay-based political party that continues to dominate politics in modern Malaysia.

Meanwhile, finding themselves shut out of public life, the communists decided that only armed struggle would lead to independence, which led the British to declare a state of Emergency in 1948. The Emergency was to last 13 years.

During this time, UMNO joined forces with two other ethnic-based political parties, the Malaysian Chinese Association (MCA) and Malaysian Indian Congress (MIC) to seek an independence acceptable to the British. After winning the first Malayan election, the alliance formed the government of the Federation of Malaya under Prime Minister Tunku Abdul Rahman in 1957, uniting all the peninsular states. Kuala Lumpur was retained as the capital. Six years later, the British colonies of Singapore, Sabah and Sarawak joined Malaya to form Malaysia, although Singapore withdrew two years later.

Shaping a Modern Malaysia

Colonial-era inequalities among Malaysians were not addressed fully at Malaysia's independence, and language and education soon became key issues of contention. In 1969, emotionally-charged elections saw a shocking erosion of the traditional majority support for the ruling alliance (now the National Front) in favour of two Chinese opposition parties. Immediately after, politically engineered bloody clashes occurred between Malays and Chinese on 13 May in Kampung Baru and Chow Kit. The violence lasted just four days, but had a long-term effect on the political landscape of Malaysia, resulting in the imposition of the controversial New Economic Policy (NEP). This aimed to address ethnic and economic inequality and to eradicate poverty by growing the economic pie. In 1970, 75 percent of Malaysians living below the poverty line were Malay, and so affirmative action for the *bumiputra* (which include Malays) became part of institutional life.

The 1970s continued to see the migration of rural populations, particularly Malays, to urban areas, including Kuala Lumpur. In 1974, KL was separated from Selangor to become a Federal Territory administered locally by the Kuala Lumpur City Hall. Skyscrapers sprung up, and, to ease overcrowding in KL, vast housing estates were built in the surrounding areas.

During the 'Asian Tiger' economic boom decade of the 1990s, the Klang Valley – and KL in particular – saw intense construction and mega pro-

Malaysia Boleh!

During the Mahathir era Malaysians became obsessed with breaking world records. Encapsulated in the clarion call of *Malaysia Boleh* (Malaysia Can Do It), these records range from the marvellous to the ridiculous; they did, however, encourage the collective pursuit of success and formed a part of the nation-building process.

jects. These were driven by the charismatic Prime Minister Mahathir Muhamad (1981–2003), whom critics decry for authoritarian rule, which included muzzling the media, judiciary and royalty, and economic policies that bred cronyism and corruption. Despite this, he put KL on the world map by building the Petronas Twin Towers in the new Kuala Lumpur City Centre, developing the Silicon Valley-type Multimedia Super Corridor, creating a brand-new federal capital at Putrajaya, and constructing the futuristic Kuala Lumpur International Airport.

The good times ended with the Asian Economic Crisis in 1997, and the furious building abated. The following year, the sacking of former Deputy Prime Minister Anwar Ibrahim sparked the largest anti-government demonstration the country had seen in 25 years. Nonetheless, Mahathir had reined in both economic and social chaos by the time he handed the government leadership to Abdullah Badawi. However, Badawi's more open governance brought to the surface dissatisfaction over abuse of the NEP and power by politicos and their business allies, as well as unhappiness over religious freedom and judicial corruption. As a result, protest votes in the 2008 elections cost the National Front its biggest ever

Flying the flag for Malaysia

number of seats, surprising the entire nation in what has been dubbed a tsunami of change. Along with five other states, KL-ites voted in a majority of opposition Members of Parliament. Nonetheless, Malaysians are now looking forward to the beginnings of the end of race-based politics and a more liberal, corruption-free and merit-based society.

Historical Landmarks

74,000BC Indigenous people settle in the Malay peninsula.

AD200 Trading with Malay archipelago, China and India begins.

AD700 The region comes under Hindu-Buddhist influences.

1300s The region comes under Islamic influences.

1400s The entrepot and Muslim sultanate of Malacca is established.

1857 Kuala Lumpur becomes a staging point for tin.

1868 Yap Ah Loy becomes *Kapitan Cina* and brings order to the town.

1874 British colonialism in the Malay peninsula begins.

1880 KL declared Selangor's capital.

1882–94 KL modernised under Frank Swettenham and Yap Ah Loy.

1895 Formation of the Federated Malay States under British rule; KL declared capital a year later.

1941–5 Japanese occupy the Malay peninsula; rise of nationalism among Malays and anti-colonialism among communist Chinese.

1948–60 State of Emergency; counter-insurgency against communists.

1955 Malaya's first national election held; the Alliance of ethnic-based political parties wins 80 percent of votes.

1957 On 31 August, Malaya is proclaimed independent, with KL as capital. Prime Minister Tunku Abdul Rahman commissions icons of statehood.

1963 Malaysia is formed, comprising Peninsular Malaysia, Singapore, Sabah and Sarawak; Singapore withdraws in 1965.

1969 Politically motivated race riots on 13 May.

1970 Nationwide New Economic Policy is introduced.

1974 KL is annexed from Selangor to become a Federal Territory.

1981 Dr Mahathir Mohamad becomes Malaysia's fourth Prime Minister.

1998 Completion of the Petronas Twin Towers and Kuala Lumpur International Airport. The economy is victim of the Asian Financial Crisis, and currency controls are imposed.

1999 Government offices moved to Putrajaya. Economy begins to rebound.

2008 Malaysia's 12th general elections result in unexpected and historic losses by the ruling political coalition and the beginnings of the move away from race-based politics.

WHERE TO GO

Explore Kuala Lumpur's old city centre first before moving on to the new city centre, then out to its green and rural outskirts. The city wears different faces in the day and at night, making some sites worth revisiting later. KL assumes a different aura again during festivities, particularly in the relevant ethnic hubs, such as Petaling Street and Bukit Bintang during Chinese New Year and Kampung Baru during the Muslim Hari Raya Puasa. To make the most of your visit, feel free to wander off and check out nooks and corners that seem interesting, though this is not always a good idea at night. Many famous sights are featured in guided bus tours, but it's often best to use trains or walk whenever possible to avoid the traffic jams.

DATARAN MERDEKA

Despite being almost smothered by tall buildings and elevated rail tracks, the historic river confluence where Kuala Lumpur was born remains intact, a tribute to the city's origins. West of the confluence is the colonial core, a collection of British-Mughal-style administrative buildings standing around the Dataran Merdeka square. Towering above them is a giant flagpole, proclamation of the country's independence.

Old Market Square

The **Old Market Square** (Medan Pasar Lama) is where the city's first brick buildings were erected in the 1880s. Bordered by Lebuh Pasar Besar and Medan Pasar, the square now hosts a busy bus stop and a clock tower, built in 1937 to commemorate the coronation of England's King George VI. A

The colonial Sultan Abdul Samad Building

wet-produce market once occupied this square, but in 1936 it was relocated about 1km (½ mile) south to Central Market *(see page 31)*, which is now a souvenir and arts complex.

Overlooking the square are several handsome **triple-storey Chinese shophouses** from the early 20th century, with neo-classical features such as columns and gables. These period shophouses are still found all over the old heart of KL and were used by families both as a home (upstairs) and to conduct business (downstairs). The shophouses are connected by continuous pedestrian verandas called five-foot ways, which really are 5ft (1.5m) wide. They originated in Singapore in 1822, the invention of colonial administrator Stamford Raffles, who deemed them essential for providing shade from the weather.

Peaceful Masjid Jamek

North of this square on Jalan Benteng you can get an excellent view of the historic confluence of the rivers Klang and Gombak. The triangular piece of land at the confluence is occupied by the graceful **Masjid Jamek** (Jamek Mosque), a sprawl of colonnades and spires. Built in 1909 in the British-Mughal style, this is the city's oldest mosque. It is open only to Muslims.

The Colonial Core
The colonial core spreads west of the confluence, girdled by Jalan Raja. This area

was the civic heart of the Federated Malay States (FMS) and, later, the Federation of Malaya, from the late 19th century until 1957, when the country gained independence from the British. The colonial architects created an institutional architectural style for the capital that combined Western neoclassical and decorative Islamic Mughal features imported from their Indian outpost. The buildings are heavily symmetrical

Saturday night life

Jalan Raja is closed to traffic every Saturday night from 7pm, and becomes a hang-out for families, youngsters and tourists taking in the bright lights illuminating the colonial buildings and Dataran Merdeka. The boulevard is also the venue for the colourful cultural parade that opens the Colours of Malaysia (Citrawarna) tourism event in May.

yet feature the liberal use of domes, arches and minarets. After independence, most of these edifices served as courts before they were recently taken over by the Ministry of National Unity, Culture, Arts and Heritage. They are undergoing renovation until the end of 2008.

At the corner of Jalan Perak and Jalan Raja is a trio of buildings. The first is the former **FMS Survey Office**, which was constructed in 1910 and sports black domes and cloverleafed arches. Adjoining it is the **Old Town Hall**, differentiated from the former by a stepped pediment. Both of these buildings have domed porches. Behind it, shaped like a wide 'V', is the **Old High Court**, distinguished by pepper-pot turrets and double-columned arches. This trio of buildings later housed the Kuala Lumpur Sessions and Magistrates Courts.

The Gombak river separates these buildings from the pièce de résistance of the colonial core, the **Sultan Abdul Samad Building** (Bangunan Sultan Abdul Samad). Stretching 137m (450ft) along Jalan Raja and anchored by a square clock tower, this vision of columns and arches was the city's

Taking a stroll in the city

first Mughal-style building. When it officially opened in 1897, KL had never seen anything like it. It served as offices for the FMS Secretariat and a host of other departments. In later times, it was the Kuala Lumpur High Court.

A lane separates the Sultan Abdul Samad Building from the **Old General Post Office**, though the two are linked by an arched bridge. The post office is distinguished by pointed arches, leaf-shaped pediments and rooftop pinnacles.

Next to this building, on the other side of the arched bridge, is the **Straits Trading Building**, which has been modernised and now houses the Industrial Court (Mahkamah Perusahaan). The court also occupies the historical building next to it, a corner pink-and-white edifice that once housed KL's first department store, **Chow Kit & Co**. The store was established in the 1890s by a KL millionaire to cater to colonials, and this site was chosen for it because it was located close to the Klang river, where supplies could easily be unloaded.

The last Mughal-style building on this side of Jalan Raja is on the other side of Jalan Medan Pasar. The orange-and-white banded building is a showcase of ornamental rectangular columns and brick. It was originally the colonial **FMS Railway Headquarters** (later the Infokraf Building).

Opposite the Sultan Abdul Samad Building is a field of green anchored at the far end by a massive flagpole. This is **Dataran Merdeka** (literally Independence Square), originally a sports field which also served as the British parade grounds. Here, on 31 August 1957, the Union flag was lowered and the new Malayan flag raised at midnight to the chimes of the clock on the Sultan Abdul Samad Building. Since independence, Dataran Merdeka has become the venue of the annual countdown to National Day (Hari Kebangsaan) as well as New Year's Day.

On the other side of the square, facing the Sultan Abdul Samad Building, are several mock-Tudor buildings. They make up the **Royal Selangor Club** (Kelab Diraja Selangor), a members-only social club frequented by high society. In colonial times, administrators, planters, merchants and their wives would gather here for a *setengah* (whisky soda) and to catch up on gossip. Although the club was founded in 1884, the current building dates back only to 1978, when it was rebuilt after a fire.

To the right of the Club, hidden by trees, is one of the region's oldest Anglican churches, the **Cathedral of St Mary the Virgin** (daily 7am–3pm; free; www.stmaryscathedral. org.my). Built in the English Gothic style, it was consecrated in 1887 and became the main place of worship for the English. The current building was built in 1922 following a fire, and features stained-glass windows that honour colonial planters and depict tropical crops such as rubber and oil palm.

Cathedral of St Mary the Virgin

At the southern end of Dataran Merdeka, on the other side of Lebuh Pasar, is the old **Chartered Bank of India, Australia and China**, with whom the colonial government held all its accounts. This 1891 three-storey period piece is bedecked with domes and arcades. It more recently housed the National History Museum, but those artefacts have been moved to the National Museum (Muzium Negara), as the building has also been taken over by the Ministry of National Unity, Culture, Arts and Heritage.

To its right is the former **Government Printing Office**, which was built around the same period as the rest of the colonial core, but sports a relatively simple neo-Renaissance design that breaks with the Mughal tradition. Some records state that its design was the original one for the Sultan Abdul Samad Building. Later, the building served as the KL Memorial Library until the new, domed **Kuala Lumpur City Library** (Perpustakaan Kuala Lumpur; Mon 2–6.45pm, Tue–Sat 9.30am–6.45pm, Sun 11am–5pm; free) was erected next to it.

Onion Domes

The onion domes used in KL's colonial architecture are the most obvious structural representation of Islam today. Found on virtually every mosque in the country, the dome was brought to the Malay archipelago by Western colonialists. Domes are believed to have first appeared in the Middle East, a roof feature that was born of expedience: the lack of timber to make flat roofs meant that mud bricks had to be used. The use of this form spread under the Byzantine Empire, and in the 7th century Arabs used this feature for the Dome of the Rock in Jerusalem, the third-most important Islamic shrine. The shape of the domes in KL's colonial core are derived from the Islamic Mughal tradition that, in turn, adopted this feature from Persian and Syrian architecture.

Railway Buildings

There is another set of lovely Mughal-style buildings about 1km (½ mile) south of the colonial core on Jalan Sultan Hishamuddin. The **Railway Administration Building** (Bangunan KTM Berhad) and the **Old KL Railway Station** (Stesen Keretapi Kuala Lumpur) are stunning architectural pieces, showcases of pillared pavilions, decorative arches and spires. While the former is still used as the offices of KTM (Malaysian Railways), the latter has been left underused since 2001, when interstate rail services were transferred to the ultra-modern KL Sentral transport

Old KL Railway Station by night

hub. Now, only KTM Komuter trains to the towns of Port Klang, Seremban and Rawang depart from here.

Central Market

Souvenir-hunters and art buffs will enjoy **Central Market** (Pasar Seni; daily 10am–10pm; www.centralmarket-kl.com. my). Located south of Old Market Square on Jalan Hang Kasturi, this was once the city's largest wet-produce market. Its Art Deco features were conserved when it was converted into a shopping mall in the 1980s. Many goods from Malaysia and Asia can be bought here, from handicrafts to clothes. Its multi-level arts space, **The Annexe**, has a varied programme of innovative performances, exhibitions and film screenings.

Petaling Street, thronged with shoppers

PETALING STREET

Of the streets in the original Chinese quarter of Kuala Lumpur, Petaling Street is the best-known among tourists. However, the whole area is worth exploring as it is full of temples, clanhouses and a bustling local community that date back to KL's origins. This enclave is still evolving, with the emergence of a new migrant social centre.

Sin Sze Si Ya Temple

One of the city's most important Taoist temples honours its most famous son, Yap Ah Loy, the Chinese community leader who prevented early KL from disappearing back into the jungle. The **Sin Sze Si Ya Temple** (daily 7am–5pm; free) is hidden from view except for a discrete doorway on Jalan Tun H.S. Lee next to Hong Leong Bank. The temple was built in 1864 by Yap himself, then the *Kapitan Cina* (Chinese Captain) of KL. He wanted to honour two of his comrades, Sin Sze Ya and Si Sze Ya, who became venerated as deities after their deaths. Their altars occupy the main hall.

After his death in 1885, Yap was also deified. The altar dedicated to him is on the left-hand side of the main hall. A bust of Yap sits nearby. If the temple seems oddly placed within its courtyard, with its entrance facing a corner, this is because it was built according to strict *feng shui* principles.

Migrant Enclave

East of this temple along Leboh Pudu and Jalan Silang is a lively social centre for Nepalis, Burmese and Bangladeshis, three large migrant worker groups. KL's economy relies heavily on an estimated 100,000 migrant workers, with the majority coming from Indonesia. This enclave provides a fascinating window into the dynamic enriching of Malaysian life and culture. Here, you will see signs which are entirely in Nepali and Burmese script. Depending on their target clientele, you will find stores stocked with Bangladeshi music and videos, *The Myanmar Times* and the sarong-like *lung ji*, or the popular Nepali fried *momo* pastry and soap and shampoo from Kathmandu. On Sundays and public holidays the area is absolutely packed.

Petitions hang in the Sin Sze Si Ya Temple

Petaling Street Bazaar

South of Jalan Tun Tan, Cheng Lock, in an area dominated by pre-war Chinese-style shophouses, is the start of the city's most famous street bazaar. Referred to by the name of the main thoroughfare which it occupies, **Petaling Street Bazaar** sits in a bustling part of KL, bookended by gateways bearing the street's name. From 10am, displays of counterfeit branded goods are laid out. You can choose from entire product lines and the latest designs off the factory floor. There are also souvenirs, fruits and munchies on sale.

By day, the stalls occupy the sidewalks in front of the shops, but from 4.30 to 11pm, the roads are closed to traffic and vendors move onto the road, which becomes one of the city's noisiest and most exciting night markets. The stalls have taken over the perpendicular Jalan Hang Lekir as well. A favoured dinner place with tourists is the stretch of Jalan Hang Lekir that leads to Jalan Sultan, which becomes bedecked in red tablecloths.

The feel of the bazaar has changed recently, as most of the stalls, once overseen by their Chinese owners, are now manned by migrant workers. This has leached the bazaar of some of its local colour, but heightened its nature as a den of cut-throat commerce. Still, bargain-hunters will enjoy themselves, although you do have to bargain hard. Non-shoppers may find the market's calmer daytime persona more manageable.

The Art of Tea

The tea shops in this area are a great place to learn about Chinese tea. Attendants will be happy to explain the different types of tea and demonstrate Chinese tea culture, less well known and elaborate than the Japanese counterpart but equally fascinating. Shops sell a range of Chinese teas, as well as porcelain and clay teapots and associated paraphernalia.

A popular tea-shop chain is **Purple Cane**, which has branches throughout the city, including at 6 Jalan Panggung, near Jalan Balai Polis (daily 11am–8pm). Purple Cane also has a restaurant (daily 11.30am–10pm) located in the Chinese Assembly Hall on Jalan Maharajalela across from the Guan Yin Temple, where every dish cooked uses Chinese tea as an ingredient.

A garland-seller on Jalan Tun H.S. Lee

Around Petaling Street

The roads around Jalan Petaling have become the city's wholesale hub of knick-knacks and fashion accessories. Nonetheless, **Jalan Sultan** retains some of the atmosphere of the old Petaling Street, with Chinese tea shops, old businesses and pre-independence eateries such as Nam Heong and Chinatown Seng Kee *(see page 137)*.

West of Jalan Petaling, the stretch of **Jalan Tun H.S. Lee** from Jalan Sultan to Jalan Hang Lekir is packed with interesting sights. At the Jalan Hang Lekir corner is the **Lee Rubber Building**, which houses Popular Bookshop. Built by one of the country's most successful rubber companies, its geometric shape and designs are classic Art Deco, a decorative architectural style that was employed throughout Malaya in the 1930s. Head upstairs to spend time at a great souvenir shop, **Peter Hoe Beyond** (daily 10am–7pm), which is also equipped with a charming café.

A Hindu priest at the Sri Maha Mariamman Temple

Diagonally opposite this building is one of the oldest Cantonese temples in the city, the **Guan Di Temple** (daily 7am–5pm; free). This 1888 place of worship honours the red-faced God of War and Literature, Guan Di, whose statue is located in the main hall. It was built by the Kwong Siew Association, a clan association representing many of Kuala Lumpur's original Cantonese-speaking Chinese families.

Opposite this temple, back on the same side as the Lee Rubber Building is a key Hindu temple, the **Sri Maha Mariamman Temple** (daily 6am–1am; free). Built in 1873, it houses a statue of the deity Murugan which is drawn on a silver chariot during the Thaipusam festival to its sister temple in Batu Caves *(see page 76)*. The temple's impressive gateway tower is adorned with intricately carved statues of Hindu deities.

South of Jalan Tun H.S. Lee is Jalan Balai Polis, home to **Gurdwara Sahib Polis** (daily 9am–5pm), a Sikh temple located within a police compound and painted in the blue of Malaysian police buildings. Sikhs were first brought from India to the Malay States by the British to be part of the police force, and once made up its majority. Opposite it is the **Old China Café** (daily 11am–10.30pm), which occupies the old guildhall of the Selangor and Federal Territory Laundry Association. It now serves Nyonya food but beautifully preserves its 1930s atmosphere, complete with wooden doors, giant *feng shui* mirrors and framed photos. Upstairs is a gallery of antiques.

Chan She Shu Yuen

At the southern end of Jalan Petaling is the **Chan She Shu Yuen Association Building** (daily 8am–5pm; free). This clan association was established in 1896 to serve early Chinese migrants to Malaya bearing the surname Chan and its variations of Chen and Tan. Although the paint has faded, this remains one of the most decorated clan association buildings in town – its roof features decorative curved gables, and its external walls are covered with remarkably detailed porcelain friezes depicting Chinese mythology, popular dramas and history.

Across the road from this building and near the pedestrian bridge across Jalan Maharajalela is a flight of steps guarded by a pair of stone lions. At the top of the stairs is the century-old **Guan Yin Temple** (daily 8am–5pm; free). This is a small Hokkien temple named after Guan Yin, the Goddess of Mercy, one of the most popular deities worshipped by local

Clanhouses

Chinese clanhouses belong to clan associations, community groups formed in the 19th century by new Chinese migrants to the country. The associations provided financial, education, employment and welfare services to newcomers, so clanhouses comprised not just temples, but accommodation and meeting halls.

Statue of the many-armed goddess of mercy, Guan Yin

Buddhists. The statue of Guan Yin here depicts her in a thousand-armed and thousand-eyed manifestation, representing her omniscience. This is one of the few Hokkien temples in town, and sports a curved roof typical of such temples.

From the side entrance of the Guan Yin Temple, steps lead to the Maharajalela Monorail Station and a car park on the left. Beyond this stands the **Stadium Merdeka**. Purpose-built to celebrate the proclamation of independence of Malaya on 31 August 1957, this humble building was the location of the most iconic moment in the country's modern history – when the first Prime Minister, Tunku Abdul Rahman, punched the air and shouted '*Merdeka*' ('independence'). The venue of great sporting events thereafter, the great boxer Muhammad Ali even fought here in 1975. The stadium has been painstakingly restored to its original shape – a triumph for conservation in development-crazy KL – and future plans include guided tours and an independence museum within its premises.

JALAN MASJID INDIA AND JALAN TAR

North of the Klang and Gombak river confluence is a chaotic, crowded and colourful enclave with a strong Indian-Muslim character. Centred around Jalan Masjid India are shops and malls selling all sorts of products from the Indian subcontinent. Parallel to this road is another old business street, Jalan Tuanku Abdul Rahman, which hosts the lively wholesale and retail fabric centre of KL.

Jalan Masjid India

Indian businesses have had a long history in KL, as is evident on Jalan Melayu (Malay Street), one of the city's original streets. One of the oldest businesses here is at No. 5 and 7, the **Goodluck Trading Company** (Mon–Sat 9am–6.30pm). This wholesale business was set up in 1895 by Indians from Chennai. The business is now run by the fourth-generation descendants of the original merchants. Their speciality is *kain pelikat chop gadja*, high-quality checked hand-loomed sarongs for men. These cloths are imported from Pulicat, an area near Chennai whose valuable textiles once funded 17th-century Dutch trade in the Malay archipelago.

Halfway along Jalan Melayu is a bazaar, which occupies the pedestrianised first stretch of Jalan Masjid India. The bazaar is fairly uninteresting, comprising Malay and Islamic knick-knacks. Shopping is better on the five-foot way of **Wisma Yakin** (daily 9am–9.30pm), on the bazaar's right, an

Men in sarongs

The cotton *kain pelikat* sarong is a favourite lounging and sleeping attire among Malaysian men, although younger urbanites have eschewed it. Malay men also wear *kain pelikat* when praying at the mosque. This is the best time to see the diversity of designs and patterns that this humble cloth comes in.

emporium of Malay shops where you can buy good local and Indonesian batiks, traditional herbal concoctions for health and beauty, and other Malay goods.

On the left of the bazaar is the brown slate-walled **Masjid India**, an Indian Muslim mosque, whose original building was erected in the 19th century and after which the street is named. Here, religious services are conducted in Arabic and Tamil, and although it is open only to Muslim worshippers, it has a unique Indian-Muslim atmosphere. At 1.30pm on Fridays, the entire bazaar area outside the mosque is filled with worshippers attending Friday prayers. There are good photo opportunities, but discretion is strongly advised.

A trader in religious goods on Jalan Masjid India

Semua House and Plaza City One

The rest of Jalan Masjid India comprises shops selling Malay outfits, scarves, *songkok* (Muslim male headgear) and sarongs, as well as Indian outfits and household products. Particularly dazzling are lavish window displays of gold jewellery in ethnic and contemporary designs that are imported from Dubai and India.

At the end of Jalan Masjid India are a couple of shopping malls. Directly facing the junction is **Semua House** (daily

10am–8pm), a one-stop shop for Malay weddings, with everything from fabrics and gift baskets to fake flowers and bridal outfits for rent. To its right, **Plaza City One** (daily 9am–10pm) is a high-rise Little India, offering traditional and Bollywood-style clothing, accessories and *mehndi* (henna-painting) services.

Opposite Plaza City One and through a car park is a massive century-old fig tree. Beneath the tree sits a tiny Hindu temple, **Sri Bathra Kaliamman Temple** (daily 6am–10pm). Its main deity is the green-faced Kali the Destroyer, but cobra-shaped worship paraphernalia in front of the temple are to appease an ancient cobra said to inhabit the fig tree. The temple is often busy as it serves as the area's place of worship for business-owners and staff.

Jalan Tuanku Abdul Rahman

Parallel to Jalan Masjid India is **Jalan Tuanku Abdul Rahman**, one of the longest streets in the city, and broad to boot. Originally called Batu Road, it was build to link pre-independence Kuala Lumpur to the tin mines in Batu. Stores sprang up along this road and it soon became the main shopping street. After independence, it was renamed after the first *Agong* (King) of Malaysia, and is fondly known as Jalan TAR.

An old-fashioned barber shop

In 1920, the **Coliseum Cinema** at No. 96 was built. Not only has the cinema survived threats to demolish it for redevelopment purposes, but it actually continues to serve its original function. Housed in a lovely neoclassical building, the cinema shows mainly Indonesian, Malay and Tamil film fare.

Next door is another institution, the **Coliseum Café and Hotel**. Built in 1928, the establishment has definitely seen better days, but its original decor and mismatched furniture and fittings are quaintly nostalgic. Its bar, now frequented by lawyers and tourists, was once a popular drinking hole for prosperous colonial planters, tin miners and traders. The upper floors once provided basic accommodation for those who did not quite make the cut for the finer hotels in the colonial quarter. It is now an atmospheric budget hotel. The restaurant (daily 10am–10pm) continues to dish up a pre-independence menu of tasty sizzling steaks and baked crab. For the former, patrons are offered tablecloth-sized napkins to keep their clothes splatter-free.

Fabric Houses

It is immediately evident that the stretch of Jalan Tuanku Abdul Rahman north of the Coliseum to the Sogo Department Store is a centre for fabrics and textiles. Almost every other shop features fabrics draped over dummies, cloth hanging from ceiling to floor, or endless shelves filled with bales of cotton, chiffon and other fluttery material. A whole gamut of stores, from retail to wholesale, has an address here.

Kamdar (daily 10am–7.30pm), a popular chain selling affordable textiles, furnishings and ready-to-wear traditional Malay and Indian clothing, has four

Tailoring

While ready-made clothing is easily available in KL, many locals still tailor their outfits. This area is full of tailors whose forte is traditional ethnic outfits, but among them are a sprinkling who can make Western-style outfits, too, for reasonable prices; some even offer a 24-hour turnaround time.

Buying sari material

outlets along this road alone (Nos 83 and 85, 113, 171, 429–35). **Gulati's Silk House** (Mon–Fri 10.30am–8.30pm, Sat 10.30am–9pm, Sun 11am–9pm), which dominates the silk market, is at No. 162/164. Its high-end chain store, **Euro Moda**, is also here at No. 126/128 (daily 10am–8.30pm). Giving Euro Moda a run for its money is **Maya's Fashion** at No. 140 (Mon–Fri 9.30am–8.30pm, Sat–Sun 11am–8.30pm). These posh outlets are where you are most likely to spot high-society *Mak Datin* (wealthy, older Malay women), starlets and politicians' wives receiving meticulous service and tailoring advice.

Besides the type of business, the common thread shared by all these stores is their Indian ownership. Most of these businesses follow in the footsteps of older establishments along the road, multi-generational family businesses that are linked to the Indian subcontinent. Sports store **G.S. Gill** at No. 106 (Mon–Fri 9.30am–6.30pm, Sat 10am–6pm, Sun

A McGill branded cricket ball

10am–5pm) was set up in 1946 to sell bicycles. Today, it is a manufacturer, licensee, wholesaler and exporter of various sporting goods, including its own brand of rackets, footballs and golf equipment (McGill). G.S. Gill himself can occasionally be seen behind the counter, keeping an eye on things.

Opposite this store is the **P. Lal Store** at No. 135 (Mon–Sat 10am–7pm), which was set up in 1929. Now run by the third generation of the family, its products continue to include high-end UK-sourced men's leather shoes, smokers' pipes and winter clothing. But it has also kept up with the times, offering online purchases and aiming to become a 'leading cyber-retailer'.

KAMPUNG BARU

Kuala Lumpur's oldest Malay settlement came into being in the 1890s as a village – Kampung Baru is literally 'New Village' in Malay. It has modernised with time, losing its original paddy fields and much of its original wooden architecture. However, the 90-hectare (220-acre) enclave has resisted the sweeping redevelopment that has long been earmarked for it, retaining a unique character that is strongly Muslim and communal. Doorways are adorned with the *asalamualaikum* welcome sign in Arabic, and children in traditional Malay dress make their way to or from religious classes. Many of the original owners have in fact moved out and rented their homes to Indonesians, particularly Javanese.

Jalan Raja Muda Musa

The gentle bustle of **Jalan Raja Muda Musa** is typical of
much of Kampung Baru. Here, the street is lined with cater-
ies which are always busy, day or night. Their customers are
mainly KL Malays, and all kinds of people, from office workers to families, come from far and wide because they know
Kampung Baru's restaurants *(see pages 138–9)* dish up the
best home-cooked Malay food in town.

Here they will find infinite variations of the rice-and-spice
nasi lemak; specialities from their home towns like the
northern *laksa*, spicy and sour rice noodles, and the east
coast *nasi kerabu* herb rice delicacy; as well as regional
favourites like the rice-and-curry *nasi padang* from Sumatra and Javanese grilled meats. Alternatively, try a snack of
local cakes or *kuih*, the most common featuring glutinous
rice, coconut milk or bananas.

White-turbaned Islamic schoolboys in Kampung Baru

The eateries are simple, with food laid out on tables and plastic chairs and tables prettied up with a vase of artificial flowers. Most are also set up in the compounds of houses, giving diners a *kampung* (village) feel. While many of Kampung Baru's houses are now partially or entirely made of brick, there are still some original stilted wooden gems to be seen. However, the ultra-modern Petronas Twin Towers in the background are a constant reminder of the transitory nature of old neighbourhoods, especially ones occupying prime land like Kampung Baru.

Jalan Raja Alang

Jalan Raja Alang, which connects to Jalan Raja Muda Musa, is a slightly quieter street. **No. 60** is a large house which is a beautiful example of traditional Malay architecture, despite being painted a garish green. It has a raised central *serambi*

Religious Schools

Kampung Baru is where you are most likely to see children attending Islamic religious schools or *madrasah*. The give-aways are their uniforms. For boys this comprises *songkok* (Malay headgear) and elasticated *sampin* (a wrap worn over trousers), and for girls, *tudung* (headscarf) and *baju kurung* (long-sleeved tunic and a sarong).

Islamic religious schools were the first educational institutions for Malays in pre-British Malaya. They were housed in vernacular-style buildings, hence their moniker of *Sekolah Pondok* (Hut School). Today, religious schools are usually confined to rural areas. Students learn subjects like Arabic and Islamic history and law. However, graduates of these schools are not recognised for entry into local universities, and must pursue tertiary education in the Middle East. The secular education system includes compulsory Islamic religious classes for Muslim students, but some urban parents send their children for supplementary religious instruction in mosques.

reception area flanked by two curving stairways and fronted by ceiling-to-floor windows for ventilation. Its compound hosts the usual food outlet.

At the corner of Jalan Raja Alang and Jalan Raja Abdullah is the **Masjid Kampung Baru** (Kampung Baru Mosque; daily 9am–5pm, except prayer times). Built around 1924, it was one of the first concrete structures erected in the quarter. It has since been renovated, and the latest addition is a gateway adorned with a turquoise ceramic pattern of Middle Eastern origin. The mosque briefly became a rallying point during the ethnic clashes of 13 May 1969 *(see page 21)*, when politically motivated trouble makers brought about its symbolic association with strife by using it as a gathering point for protests.

Friday worshippers at the
Masjid Kampung Baru

Fortunately, peace now reigns at the mosque, and it has become more famous for feeding the masses. During the Muslim fasting month of Ramadan, the mosque dishes out endless bowls of *bubur lambuk*, a peppery rice porridge cooked with minced beef. The massive cook-out was initiated by two imams in the 1950s and is part of community service by the area's residents. Ramadan is a particularly lively time to visit this street, as a riot of mainly food stalls beneath colourful umbrellas do a roaring trade during the month-long **Pasar Ramadan**,

One of Guru Nanak Darbaar Gurdwara Sahib's domes

literally 'Ramadan Market' (3pm–midnight). The atmosphere is festive as Muslims throng the market to buy home speciality Ramadan delicacies or break fast *(buka puasa)* there during the evening *maghrib* prayer time around 7.30pm. The date of Ramadan changes each year, as it follows the lunar calendar.

One would have thought that a Sikh temple would be out of place in a largely Muslim neighbourhood; but not in KL. The presence of the impressive **Guru Nanak Darbaar Gurdwara Sahib** on Jalan Alang, west of the Kampung Baru Mosque, is yet another testament to the cultural and religious tolerance practised by Malaysians (although it is strictly open only to worshippers). On its roof are squat Indo-Persian domes, adorned at the base with lotus petals; this design predates the Mughal domes adopted by the British for the colonial core. The central dome has a miniature umbrella called a *chatri*, symbolising shelter for mankind. Its main prayer hall is the largest in Southeast Asia.

Chow Kit Market

Next to the Sikh temple is the **Chow Kit Market** (daily 6am–8pm), one of the largest and oldest traditional fresh-produce markets in the city. Its Raja Alang boundary is marked by a plethora of fruit stalls (daily 24 hours). Depending on the season, you will find fresh tropical fruits like durian, rambutan and jackfruit. Inside the market is a chaotic rabbit warren of narrow, congested alleyways, often damp. Spices and herbs used in Malay cooking are plentiful here, as well as cooked Malay food in addition to fresh fish, meat, vegetables and sundries.

Diagonally opposite the market across Jalan Tuanku Abdul Rahman is **Jalan Haji Taib**, the location of the Malay version of the Petaling Street bazaar (Mon–Sat 4–11pm, Sun noon–midnight). While there are cheap goods on sale here, the atmosphere is sleazier; beware of pickpockets, especially at night. On sale are reject clothing from factories, second-hand denims from the US and Japan, and goods from Thailand.

Titiwangsa

Located in the neighbourhood of Titiwangsa northwest of Kampung Baru is the **National Art Gallery** (Balai Senilukis Negara; daily 10am–6pm; free). This beautiful contemporary space elegantly incorporates elements of traditional

The clean lines of the National Art Gallery

Malay architecture in a multi-storey 13,000-sq m (140,000-sq ft) space. Of its six galleries, the ground-floor main gallery showcases works from the institution's 2,500-piece permanent collection. New exhibitions are held every three months.

Next door to the art gallery and overshadowing it is a less successful architectural structure, the **National Theatre** (Istana Budaya). Looking like an overblown Malay house, the National Theatre hosts large-scale local and international productions. Each Saturday night (8pm–midnight), the car park between these two buildings sees a carnival-like cultural event, **Laman Santai,** with colourful arts and craft stalls and traditional performances.

Behind these buildings is a popular urban park called the **Titiwangsa Lake Gardens** (Taman Tasik Titiwangsa; 24 hours; free). Spread over 46 hectares (114 acres), the park is popular with picnickers, joggers and for boating. Horse-riding within an enclosed paddock is available at weekends.

Near the park at 12 Persiaran Titiwangsa 3 is **Sutra House** (tel: 03-4022 9669; www.sutradancetheatre.com), a dance school owned by renowned classical Indian dance exponent Ramli Ibrahim. The grounds also house a charming landscaped outdoor stage where Indian dance and music recitals are held from time to time.

LAKE GARDENS AND BRICKFIELDS

West of the colonial core spreads a 104-hectare (257-acre) urban park called the Lake Gardens. A green and peaceful oasis for the residents of Kuala Lumpur, here pathways meander through lawns, cultivated gardens and animal sanctuaries, as well as museums. South of the Lake Gardens is the atmospheric old neighbourhood of Brickfields, home to a mainly Indian community and an impressive number of places of worship.

Lake Gardens

The brainchild of a former British State Treasurer 130 years ago, the **Lake Gardens** (Taman Tasik Perdana; daily 24 hours; free) has become an important recreation area and green lung in a built-up cityscape. Dawn and dusk witness a host of exercise enthusiasts, from joggers to t'ai chi exponents, and weekends draw mums, dads and kids, with maids in tow and picnic baskets in hand; this is a good opportunity to watch Malaysian families at play.

Flora and Fauna

The main artery through the gardens is Jalan Cenderawasih, which leads to most of the attractions. East of this road is Jalan Cenderasari and the **Butterfly Park** (daily 9am–6pm; charge). Here, in pretty surroundings, an extremely humid environment keeps thousands of plants and butterflies of all shapes and colours happy.

Early birds

An early start to the day enables visitors to enjoy the gardens while it is cooler and the greenery fresher. Visitors who reach the gardens by 7am can even participate in the numerous t'ai chi sessions held there, usually led by volunteers and open to all.

West of Jalan Cenderawasih, Jalan Tembusu leads to the **lake**, which isn't much to look at, although you can hire paddleboats to go on it (Mon–Fri 10am–noon, 3–5pm, Sat–Sun

In the Butterfly Park

and public holidays 9am–noon, 2.30–5pm; rental fee). Worth visiting near the lake is the **Conservatory and Herbal Garden** (daily 9am–6pm; free). While the Conservatory showcases beautifully laid-out plant collections, including luxurious heliconia and ginger collections, the herbal section provides insights into local herbs and spices.

Next to the path to the lake is also the walkway to the **Hibiscus Garden** (daily 9am–6pm; free Mon–Fri). The garden is a tribute to the hibiscus *(bunga raya)*, the national flower, and features 2,500 hibiscus plants from all over the world. A pathway at the back of this garden leads to the **Orchid Garden** (daily 9am–6pm; free Mon–Fri). Malaysia has among the most diverse orchid species in the world, and this garden shows off a mixture of wild and cultivated species, of which some specimens are for sale.

Opposite the Orchid Garden is the **Kuala Lumpur Bird Park** (daily 9am–6pm; charge). This 8-hectare (20-acre) covered aviary is home to over 200 bird species, most housed in display areas. Do not miss the hornbill section, where you can get close-up views of these large black-and-white creatures with prominent beaks and magnificent tails.

Jalan Cenderawasih ends in a T-junction, the right branch of which leads to the **Deer Park** (Mon–Thur 10am–noon, 2–6pm, Fri 10am–noon, 3–6pm, Sat–Sun 10am–6pm; free). This is a rare opportunity to view the mouse deer, the world's smallest deer, which is the size of a cat, and extremely shy. The park's breeding success has been high, so lucky visitors might just spot a baby. Visitors may also feed Mauritian and Dutch deer here.

The Edges of Lake Gardens

West of the lake on Persiaran Mahameru is an elegant pair of colonial mansions called **Carcosa Seri Negara**, now a luxury boutique hotel (www.ghmhotels.com). The mock-Tudor Carcosa, which was built in 1896, was once the residence of top British officials. The other mansion, the Seri Negara, sits on an adjoining hill. Cool down with a beer in the hotel's bar or partake in Devonshire tea on its verandas (daily 3–6pm).

South of the gardens on Jalan Damansara is the **National Museum** (Muzium Negara; daily 9am–6pm), a fine example of post-independence architecture. The museum is undergoing renovations and should reopen in 2009.

At the southeastern end of the Lake Gardens on Jalan Lembah Perdana is the **Islamic Arts Museum Malaysia** (Muzium Kesenian Islam Malaysia; daily 10am–6pm; charge; www.iamm.org.my), which has a fine collection of artefacts and art objects, many from the Middle Eastern Islamic world. The building itself is a beauty, a dignified contemporary space that incorporates Iranian and Central Asian architecture.

National Monument

North of the Lake Gardens across Jalan Parliament is the National Monument (Tugu Negara; daily, 24 hours; free), which commemorates servicemen who died during the communist insurgency of 1948–60. It was modelled after the Iwo Jima Memorial in the US. Steps lead down to a cenotaph commemorating the soldiers of the two World Wars.

Down the hill is the ASEAN Sculpture Garden (daily 24 hours; free), whose sculptures symbolise the mainly economic alliance among the 10 nations of the Association of Southeast Asian Nations.

Next to this museum is the **Masjid Negara** (National Mosque; Mon–Thur 9am–noon, 3–4pm, 5.30–6.30pm, Fri for Muslim worshippers only; free). Completed in 1965, it was one of the first buildings built to reflect statehood. It sports a unique circular blue-ridged roof symbolising an open umbrella, geometric latticework and white marble.

Brickfields

South of the Lake Gardens is Brickfields. The area was thus named because it was here in the late 19th century

The geometric Masjid Negara

that clay was dug up and bricks manufactured to rebuild Kuala Lumpur after fires and floods destroyed the settlement's wooden buildings. After that, Brickfields became a centre for the railways and government quarters for local civil servants. Since most colonial railway workers and civil servants were Tamils from South India and Sri Lanka, the area has an Indian flavour. The northern claypit is being redeveloped into the ultra-modern railway hub of KL Sentral, a self-contained city of offices, condominiums and hotels.

Jalan Scott and Jalan Thambipillay

Jalan Scott is where the Brickfields township first took shape. An important Hindu temple here is the **Sri Kandaswamy Kovil** (daily 5am–1pm, 5–9pm; free), which was founded by the local Jaffna Sri Lankan community in 1909. This is a Murugan temple which sports an impressive gateway and marble and gold fittings. Down the road from it is the humble **Arulnegu Sree Veera Hanuman Temple**, which honours an uncommon deity – Hanuman, the Monkey God (daily 7am–10pm; free). Best-known from the epic *Ramayana*, Hanuman is revered for courage and devotion. This temple houses five statues of the deity, and Saturdays are especially busy here. Among the old shophouses along this street, **Wei-Ling Gallery** at No. 8 shows a beautiful reuse of space after the shophouse was gutted by fire (Mon–Fri noon–7pm, Sat 10am–5pm). This art gallery sells contemporary local and international art.

Southwest of Jalan Scott is **Jalan Thambipillay**, which runs through a busier part of Brickfields. A notable feature here is the large number of blind people; they frequent the Malaysian Association of the Blind, which is next to the Tun Sambanthan Monorail station. Some are trained masseurs who work in the massage parlours along Jalan Thambipillay. There is a 50-year-old Buddhist temple here called the **Three Teachings Temple**, whose back faces the road. Surprisingly, located next to it is a red-light area in the shape of a dozen seedy shop lots.

Intricately carved deities at the Sri Kandaswamy Kovil

Jalan Berhala

Jalan Thambipillay leads to **Jalan Berhala**, a U-shaped road formerly known as Temple Road, which is packed with pre-World War II places of worship, as well as a host of schools, bungalows and flats. A key temple here is the **Sri Sakti Karpaga Vinayagar Temple** (daily

Petals in Maha Vihara Temple

6am–noon, 6–9.30pm; free). It is the country's only temple hosting the Elephant God Ganesha holding a Sivalingam, a symbol synonymous with the principal god Siva. During the festival celebrating Ganesha, which falls in the Tamil month of Aavani (Aug–Sept), this statue is drawn by elephants in a chariot around Brickfields. Round the corner from this temple is another unexpected sight, the local pub in the shape of a zinc-roofed **toddy shop**. Toddy, the fermented sap of young coconut, is cheap booze that has always been disreputable, which is why the shop is almost enclosed by a wall.

Further down Jalan Berhala is the **Maha Vihara Temple** (daily 5.30am–10.30pm; free), one of KL's most important Buddhist temples, founded by Singhalese who were brought here by the British to be civil servants. Modest in appearance, the temple assumes an electric atmosphere come Wesak Day (May), which marks the birth, enlightenment and death of the Buddha. This temple is the start and end point of a night-time float procession featuring hundreds of devotees.

Other Landmarks

Other landmarks in this area include the **Hundred Quarters** on Jalan Chan Ah Tong and Jalan Rozario. Set in straight rows, these 1915 British-built quarters housed middle-class civil servants, and are built of concrete, then considered a luxury. Barely changed over the years, they continue to house a lively multi-ethnic community of civil servants. Fronting Jalan Tun Sambanthan is the **Vivekenanda Ashram**, established for followers of the influential spiritual leader of the Vedanta branch of Hindu philosophy. A statue of Vivekenanda stands in front of this long pink-and-white building. West of this building on Jalan Tun Sambanthan and Jalan Travers are rows of **shophouses** offering everything from carnatic music to Indian mangoes and lovely South Indian banana-leaf meals.

Many churches are found in this area, representing a large array of denominations, including the Catholic Church of the Holy Rosary, the Tamil Methodist Church, the Zion Lutheran Cathedral and Our Lady of Fatima Church, where services are held in English as well as Tamil and/or Mandarin. An interesting edifice is the **St Mary's Orthodox Syrian Cathedral** on Jalan Tun Sambanthan Satu (daily 9am–7pm; free; www.mymalankara.com). This faith has origins in Kerala, and this church was the first church in the order to be consecrated outside India in 1958.

Just a few of the Hundred Quarters

The Golden Triangle is particularly beautiful by night

KLCC

Soaring 452m (1,483ft) into the sky, the iconic Petronas Twin Towers are the literal high point of the city and of Kuala Lumpur's new heart, the Kuala Lumpur City Centre (KLCC). Like KL Sentral, this 40-hectare (100-acre) area is a redevelopment exercise, occupying what used to be the Selangor Turf Club. This self-contained city will eventually comprise tower blocks serving as corporate offices, hotels and luxury accommodation, all surrounding an artily landscaped park. KLCC anchors the city's business and financial district, called the Golden Triangle, and is the place to find the best shopping and nightlife.

Petronas Twin Towers

Clad entirely in steel and glass, the **Petronas Twin Towers** (www.klcc.com.my) are quite an amazing sight, especially at night against the velvet night sky. Full-moon nights are particularly mesmerising, and, if you get your vantage point right, the yellow orb appears suspended between the lighted spires. The Twin Towers were built at the end of the Mahathir administration as a monument that would befit an economic Asian Tiger nation making its presence felt in the world. The towers did hold the Guinness Book of Records' world's tallest building record between 1996 and 2003, after which the Taipei 101 Tower topped it by 56m (190ft). They remain among the tallest structures in the world.

A breathtaking piece of engineering that consumed unimaginable amounts of concrete, steel and glass, the Twin Towers' architecture, by the renowned New York-based Cesar Pelli, also encapsulates Malaysian sensibilities. The basic shape of each tower is an eight-point star formed from two interlocking squares, a popular Islamic architectural design. Semi-circles are superimposed on the inner angles of the squares. Steel sections working as sun-shading devices add to the unique lines and shadows on the buildings' facades. There are 88 storeys in all, signifying 'double luck', a Chinese belief.

The Twin Towers house offices, including the headquarters of state oil and gas giant Petronas, but are not open to the public. However, sightseers may visit the **Skybridge** (Tue–Sun 9am–7pm; free; maximum 1,600 tickets per day), a double-decked passageway linking the towers on the 41st and 42nd floors. There isn't much of a view from here, but queues are long and start as early as 8am on the concourse level of Tower Two. This level is also the location of the box office of the custom-built **Petronas Philharmonic Hall** (Dewan Filharmonik Petronas; Mon–Sat 10am–6pm, 9pm on performance days, noon to

Cheap tickets

Matinée tickets for the Malaysian Philharmonic Orchestra can go for as little as RM10. The concert programme also includes interesting and popular concerts for children.

Enjoying the Petrosains museum

performance time on performance Sun; box office tel: 03-2051 7007; www.malaysianphilharmonic.com; dress codes apply). The interesting programme features not only the Malaysian Philharmonic Orchestra but international musicians ranging from chamber and contemporary classical to jazz and world music.

Suria KLCC

The base of the towers is occupied by a classy six-storey shopping centre, **Suria KLCC** (daily 10am–10pm), which has over 270 speciality shops and restaurants as well as cinemas and other attractions. Most of the Malaysiana souvenir and gift shops as well as boutiques are located on Levels 2 and 3. Among these is the **Pucuk Rebung Royal Gallery-Museum** at 302-A, set up by a serious antique-collector who has laid out a museum-like space of precious personal and for-sale Malaysian and regional artefacts, antiques and objets d'art. Next door to Pucuk Rebung is an elegant art gallery, **Galeri Petronas** (Tue–Sun 10am–8pm; www.galeripetronas. com), known for its expertly curated exhibitions.

Petronas also runs an excellent interactive museum on science and the oil and gas industry for families. **Petrosains** (Tue–Sun 9.30am–5.30pm; charge; www.petrosains.com.my) is located on the sixth floor. On the ground floor is another beautifully laid out, if commercial, gallery of Southeast Asian handicrafts and products, **Aseana** (G13-19). At the front of the shopping centre is an esplanade which faces a choreographed fountain display, especially pretty when night-lit.

The esplanade is also lined with trendy cafés and bars, great for people-watching over a latte or wine. A view of the fountains and esplanade can also be had from the upstairs restaurants on this side of Suria.

KLCC Park

The fountains sit in a lake within the lovely **KLCC Park** (daily 7am–10pm), a 20-hectare (50-acre) garden designed by the late Brazilian landscape artist Roberto Burle Marx. Among the vegetation are about 40 trees which date back to the time when the area was the Selangor Turf Club. There is also a jogging track, sculptures, a playground and wading pool (Tue–Fri 10am–7.30pm), and in the northeast corner the Uzbek-inspired **Masjid Asy-Syakirin** (Asy-Syakirin Mosque; daily 9am–5pm, except prayer times), featuring a metallic dome and delicate Islamic calligraphy.

View over KLCC Park

In the southeast part of the KLCC is the Kuala Lumpur Convention Centre, where concerts and theatre performances are sometimes staged. Its concourse level is occupied by the **Aquaria KLCC** (daily 11am–8pm, last admission at 7pm; charge; www.klaquaria.com). This family-oriented aquarium is stocked with over 5,000 fish and other marine life; it also has a rainforest exhibition.

Nightlife Hubs

The Petronas Twin Towers are surrounded by some of the best **nightlife** in Southeast Asia. The zigzagging streets of Jalan Sultan Ismail, Jalan P. Ramlee and Jalan Pinang are packed with clubs, pubs and restaurants such as Poppy Collection, Rum Jungle, Beach Club, Espanda and that oldie-but-goodie, the Hard Rock Café. Meanwhile, Jalan Ampang's jewel is **Zouk,** which encases several clubs in an iconic egg-shaped structure. Jalan Doraisamy, west of KLCC, is home to the swanky **Asian Heritage Row**, a row of wonderfully renovated pre-war shophouses that are now occupied by among the fanciest eateries and watering holes in town.

KL Tower

Because the highest point of the Petronas Twin Towers is closed to the public, the best place to get a bird's-eye view of Kuala Lumpur is the **KL Tower** (Menara Kuala Lumpur; daily 9am–10pm; charge; www.menarakl.com.my). Located

Top Views

Visitors often like to photograph the Petronas Twin Towers from the Suria Esplanade, but the best views of the towers are from the KLCC Park, Jalan Ampang, Jalan Tun Razak and the hotels around it. Stunning night-time views are on offer from chic rooftop bars like the Luna Bar at the Pacific Regency Hotel Suites, the Sky Lounge at Hotel Maya (hotel guests only) and the Sky Lounge at the Trader's Hotel.

The best views of the KL skyline are actually from the Kuala Lumpur Elevated Highway, parallel to Jalan Ampang, where you can see both of the city's iconic towers; note, though, that pedestrians are not allowed on the highway and drivers are not allowed to stop.

The best times to photograph the Twin Towers are during the spectacular fireworks displays on New Year's Eve and National Day (31 Aug).

The spectacular view from KL Tower's Observation Deck

west of the Twin Towers on the Bukit Nanas hill, the KL Tower is, in fact, actually about 60m (197ft) taller than the former when measured from sea level because of its elevated location. Sporting a typical telecommunications tower design, the KL Tower comprises a huge shaft rising from the ground topped by a circular six-storey head, whose design is inspired by the traditional Malay spinning top *(gasing)*. The public **Observation Deck** is located on the first level of the tower head and, weather permitting, is the best place to view the upper reaches of the Petronas Twin Towers as well as the city. Binoculars and a good audio tour help enrich the visitor's viewing experience. The building also contains souvenir shops, an amphitheatre, cafés and a revolving restaurant. Queues can be long during the school holidays.

The KL Tower has also been styling itself as an extreme sports venue. From the ground floor, a **'flying fox'** winches

Giant Jelutong

A magnificent century-old Jelutong tropical hardwood tree located right by the KL Tower takes pride of place in this attraction; during the tower's construction, a RM430,000 retaining wall was built around it to protect it.

visitors down on an inclined 100m (330ft) long rope. Two annual events at the KL Tower also draw a good crowd: the Kuala Lumpur International Forest Towerthon (basically a run up Bukit Nanas and the tower) and the Kuala Lumpur Tower International Jump, which involves BASE jumping (parachute-aided free-falling). Activity dates are posted on the KL Tower website.

Bukit Nanas Park

The hill on which the KL Tower sits is the country's oldest forest reserve, gazetted in 1906 and purportedly the forest in which indigenous Orang Asli once hunted. The Orang Asli have long since moved out, and the reserve has been turned into the **Bukit Nanas Forest Recreational Park** (daily 7am–6pm). Despite being surrounded by concrete and glass, it is surprisingly lush and species-rich. Five short and well-marked trails have been developed, but visitors should check in first at the Forest Information Centre on Jalan Raja Chulan. The KL Tower also conducts free 45-minute tours of the park, starting from the tower's ground floor (11am, 12.30pm, 2.30pm and 4.30pm).

In the western foothills of Bukit Nanas are two of Kuala Lumpur's best-achieving schools, housed in beautiful classical buildings. Built in English Gothic style, the all-girls **Convent Bukit Nanas** at the northern end of Jalan Bukit Nanas was established in 1899 by French Catholic nuns and was the city's first convent school. Its brother school down the road, **St John's Institution**, was established in 1904. Its main block is a brick-red Grecian-Spanish-influenced structure, among the most elaborate school buildings in KL.

Next to the boys' school is the dignified **Cathedral of St John** (daily 6am–6.30pm; free), which was built in 1883 and serves as the central Peninsular Malaysian Roman Catholic church. It has a large Filipino congregation, and Sundays see the setting up of stalls around the church selling Filipino snacks, books and VCDs.

Down the hill from the cathedral and hugging the Lorong Ampang-Jalan Raja Chulan corner is the **National Telecommunications Museum** (Muzium Telekom Negara; Tue–Sun 9am–5pm). Its exhibits are not inspiring, but the building is one of the finest examples of neoclassical architecture in the city, complete with imposing columns and perfect proportions. It originally housed the Central Battery Manual Telephone Exchange.

Following the trails through Bukit Nanas Park

The bright lights and bustle of Bukit Bintang

BUKIT BINTANG

Centred around Jalan Bukit Bintang, the Bukit Bintang area is packed with shopping centres, hotels, eateries and nightlife venues. Bukit Bintang ('Star Hill') was the undisputed centre of entertainment in 1950s Kuala Lumpur. However, over the years congestion, grime and vice set in, until 1999, when visionary property mogul Francis Yeoh turned it around in a multi-million-Ringgit remodelling exercise. Other building-owners soon followed suit, and today the entire area is a vibrant, exciting attraction, with a constant flow of bodies, from corporate types to the *nouveau* rich.

Bintang Walk

The masterstroke that saved Bukit Bintang from decrepitude is a 1km (½-mile) long promenade known as **Bintang Walk**. Modelled after Paris's Avenue des Champs-Elysées, the broad walkway is lined with sidewalk cafés, ice-creameries, shops and restaurants. Most of the properties on this strip, which runs from the Westin Hotel to the Lot 10 mall, were also bought by Francis Yeoh's company, YTL Corp, and given a new lease of life. Among them is the David Rockwell, New York-designed **Starhill Gallery** (daily 10am–9.30pm; www.starhillgallery.com), the first luxury shopping centre in the city. Linked to sister properties the J.W. Marriott Hotel and The Ritz-Carlton, it features separate dedicated product floors which are accessed in the lifts by their names rather than numbers. A basement Feast Village and top-level art-gallery floor sandwich Louis Vuitton and Dior concept mega-stores and other branded shops. A unique string of boutiques in this shopping centre feature highly specialised collectors' watches and jewellery.

There are two other shopping centres along Bintang Walk. **Kuala Lumpur Plaza** (daily 11am–10pm) is anchored by American chain restaurant Planet Hollywood and houses innovative local couturier Bernard Chandran. The landmark green **Lot 10** (daily 10am–9.30pm) is a fashionable, upmarket hang-out whose main tenant is the Japanese-owned Isetan department store. It has an excellent food court where you can sample street food in air-conditioned comfort.

Recently, the face of Bukit Bintang drastically changed again with the official opening of the **Pavilion Kuala Lumpur** (daily 10am–10pm; www.pavilion-kl.com). Located opposite Starhill, it boasts, like Starhill, exclusive local and international de-

Street parties

Bukit Bintang frequently hosts street parties, when the roads are closed to traffic, and concerts and fireworks displays are staged. Occasions to look out for include New Year's Eve, Chinese New Year and the Sepang Formula One weekend. Check details with Tourism Malaysia.

signer boutiques, eateries, art galleries, and health and beauty stores. The difference is that these are sprawled over seven levels and almost 130,000 sq m (1.4 million sq ft) of street-front retail shops. But this monolith is just the tip of the commercial-space iceberg; the ongoing construction will eventually result in a 'self-contained' enclave of office blocks, residential towers and a luxury hotel.

Sungei Wang Plaza and Bukit Bintang Plaza

Across the Jalan Sultan Ismail junction is an older, more sober part of the Bukit Bintang shopping area. Bargain-hunters will appreciate the linked shopping centres of **Bukit Bintang Plaza** (daily 10.30am–10pm) and **Sungei Wang Plaza** (daily 10am–10pm), whose entrance actually faces Jalan Sultan Ismail. Because most of the shops in these malls are small and their turnover quick, competition is stiff, which keeps prices low. Cool teenage gear is available at the T-Hop zone on Level 6 of Sungei Wang, while audio-visual equipment and cameras are good buys in the Bukit Bintang Plaza. The real draw of these shopping centres, though, is clothing, and the variety is mind-boggling, ranging from the latest hip-hop and Taiwanese fashion to quality Malaysian-made

Wooing Shoppers

The presence of the Pavilion Kuala Lumpur has notched up the competition among the shopping centres, not only in Bukit Bintang, but throughout KL. Therefore, activities and promotions are becoming crucial in attracting customers. Shopping centres are especially fun to visit during the festive seasons of Chinese New Year, Hari Raya, Deepavali and Christmas, with innovative decorations, activities galore and seasonal goodies for sale. Meanwhile, the Mega Sale Carnival period from May to August serves up some great bargains.

The enormous Berjaya Times Square mall

T-shirts and jeans. Accessories, shoes, cosmetics, toiletries and leather goods are also plentiful.

For diehard shopaholics, the largest mall in town is **Berjaya Times Square** on Jalan Imbi (daily 10am–10pm), but the products here tend to be of lower quality. The mall also has a cineplex, IMAX theatre, bowling alley and an indoor theme park. Kuala Lumpur is also a great place to buy computers and computer accessories. Most shopping centres have an IT section, but the best buys are in the dedicated IT malls of **Plaza Low Yat** and **Imbi Plaza**, both open daily from 10am to 10pm.

Ain Arabia

North of Bukit Bintang Plaza is **Ain Arabia**, a little Arab quarter along Jalan Berangan. Here you'll find Middle Eastern restaurants, barbers and hairdressing salons, a mini market, souvenir shops and travel agents. The Sahara Tent restaurant near Fortuna Hotel has become a focal point of the enclave, with a range of Middle Eastern cuisine, Moorish arches and tinkling fountains, as well as private booths for women in *burqas* (veiled outer garment) to dine in private.

Ain Arabia was set up to provide a 'home away from home' for tourists from the Gulf region whom Malaysia has been seriously wooing. Since 2003, Muslim-friendly Malaysia has been seeing double-digit growth rates in the number of Arab tourists, many of whom are facing immigration difficulties travelling outside of the Middle East in a post-9/11 world. Malaysian hospitality to them starts at the Kuala Lumpur International Airport with services like Arabic announcements and a special immigration lane for Arab tourists with families. The peak period for Middle Eastern tourists – mostly honeymooners and families – is from June to September.

Jalan Conlay

While some Malaysian souvenirs are available for sale in Bukit Bintang, the place to go to for a wide range of local products is a little bit away from the main shopping area. Northeast of Bukit Bintang along the quiet Jalan Conlay is the **Kuala Lumpur Craft Complex** (Kompleks Kraf Kuala Lumpur; daily 9am–8pm; free; www.kraftangan.gov.my). This 'one-stop craft centre' – a more upmarket version of the Central Market – has on sale quality Malaysian arts and crafts from all over the coun-

Craft Expo

Each year at the end of Feb/early Mar, the Kuala Lumpur Craft Complex hosts a week-long festival of handicraft from all over Malaysia. Visitors will get the chance to speak to handicraft-makers, buy their products and see craft-making demonstrations. There are also cultural performances. For details, tel: 03-2162 7459.

Shopping in the Kuala Lumpur Craft Complex

try, including basketry, textiles, silverware and pottery. Visitors might also want to check out its **Craft Museum** (daily 9am–5.30pm; charge) or set aside a few hours to have a go at making their own batik artwork, pottery or woodcraft in its **Craft Village** (fee applies). In the **Artists' Colony** (daily 10am–6pm), up-and-coming Malaysian artists can be seen at their canvasses. They are generally open to a chat and certainly to purchases.

Near this complex, at the junction of Jalan Stonor, is the **Heritage of Malaysia Trust** (Badan Warisan Malaysia; Mon–Sat 10am–5.30pm; free; www.badanwarisan.org.my). This non-governmental organisation works mainly through advocacy and education towards the preservation and conservation of the country's architectural heritage. The Trust is housed in a 1925 colonial bungalow and has a small but excellent gift shop whose products range from books to cards and collectables. Visitors may also browse

Ruhman Penghulu Abu Seman

its resource centre (Tue–Sat 10am–4pm, by appointment; charge).

Not to be missed is a tour of the **Rumah Penghulu Abu Seman**, a beautiful traditional Malay house which sits in the Trust's grounds. An increasingly rare sight throughout the country, this all-timber house, formerly owned by a village headman, was relocated from the northern state of Kedah to Kuala Lumpur and restored by the organisation as an awareness-raising and conservation project (tours Mon–Sat 11am and 3pm; charge; book ahead).

Jalan Alor and Changkat Bukit Bintang

One of the best places to sample local Chinese hawker food is **Jalan Alor**. Lined with eateries, this street's pavements are overtaken by a host of fluorescent-lit food stalls and rickety tables and stools come evening. You get the gamut of Chinese fare here, from simple noodle dishes to more adventurous foods like venison and tripe. Just walk along the street and stop when you see something that takes your fancy.

More good food is dished up at stalls along the parallel **Tengkat Tong Shin**, some of which have been around for decades. However, their continued existence cannot be guaranteed. The success of the main Jalan Bukit Bintang strip might have resuscitated commerce, but other consequences include rising rental costs and the influx of property investors keen on a piece of the pie. Subsequently, old families from this neighbourhood have been leaving the area. Many of the remaining pre-war houses along Tengkat Tong Shin have been turned into restaurants, pubs or 'flashpackers' – higher-end backpacker accommodation. This street has already become a centre for budget accommodation.

Meanwhile, trendy has really colonised the perpendicular **Changkat Bukit Bintang**. Watering holes and international restaurants are de rigueur here. Among local favourites are the Cuban salsa outfit Little Havana, the elegant Japanese jazz bar Yoko's, and the hot-and-happening gay bar, Frangipani, which also serves delicious French food. For great live local acts, check out No Black Tie at 17 Jalan Mesui (daily 6pm–2am, longer at weekends; showtime from 10pm). Run by a classical pianist, this cosy club and restaurant pioneered performing space for upcoming singer/songwriters and remains a favourite among them.

Hawker food on sale on Jalan Alor

A beautiful orchid at the
Conservatory of Rare Plants

DAY TRIPS

Kuala Lumpur is a great jump-off for day trips. From museums and cave temples to lush forests and historic estuaries, the options are plentiful and varied. Tourists should try driving outside KL, as the roads and highways are in good condition and go through interesting small towns and rural landscapes.

Museum of Asian Art and Rimba Ilmu

Located in Kuala Lumpur's southwest corner, bordering Petaling Jaya, are two wonderful attractions within Universiti Malaya, the oldest university in the country. The **Museum of Asian Art** (Muzium Seni Asia; Mon–Fri 9am–5pm, Fri closed 12.15–2.45pm; free) is a gem showcasing 6,000 pieces of art – mainly ceramics – spanning 4,000 years of history in Malaysia and Asia. Book ahead for a guided tour.

Rimba Ilmu ('Forest of Knowledge') is a tropical botanical garden and one of the most important biological conservatories in Malaysia (Mon–Thur 9am–1pm, 2–4pm, Fri 9am–noon, 2.45–4pm; charge; http://rimba.um.edu.my). It has an excellent interpretive exhibition on rainforests and the environment, a rainforest garden featuring five core collections, including medicinal plants, palms and citrus species, and, for guided tours only, the exquisite **Conservatory of Rare Plants and Orchids**, comprising 1,700 plants that are rare or are becoming rare, including begonia, orchids and giant 'umbrella leaf' palms.

Sunway Lagoon

Families love the **Sunway Lagoon Water Theme Park** (Mon, Wed–Fri 11am–6pm, Sat–Sun and school holidays 10am–6pm, closed public holidays; charge; www.sunway. com.my). Spread over 32 hectares (80 acres), it has four different themed parks packed with rides and the world's largest man-made surf beach, complete with artificial waves. A great view of the park can be had from the **Sunway Pyramid** next door (daily 10am–10pm), an Egyptian-themed shopping centre anchored by a giant lion in a sphinx pose.

Batu Caves

About half an hour's drive north of the city centre is the Sri Subramaniar Swamy or **Batu Caves Temple**, home to a cave temple halfway up a limestone massif. Hindu devotees started praying at this cave temple in 1891, when the only deity worshipped there was Murugan, represented by his *vel* (trident). Today that *vel* still sits in the **Temple Cave**, along with the statues of several other deities (daily 7.30am–1pm, 4–8.30pm; free). The cave itself is magnificent, an 80 by 100m (260 by 330ft) chamber bedecked with stalactites and stalagmites, and opening at one end into a skylight.

Batu Caves Temple

These days, Murugan is also represented by a 43m (140ft) tall **gilded statue of Murugan**, the largest of its kind in the world. It stands at the bottom of the stairs to the Temple Cave. The rest of the temple complex comprises shrines to a host of other deities, as well as cave galleries containing traditional Indian art (daily 6am–9pm; charge for galleries only).

Batu Caves is particularly important for celebrants of the Hindu festival of repentance called **Thaipusam** at the end of January. A remarkable sensory experience, over a million devotees converge here to offer Murugan thanks and prayers, many offering acts of penance such as the carrying of large structures called *kavadi* or piercing their bodies with sharp spokes. The festival begins with the bearing of an important statue of Murugan here from the Sri Maha Mariamman Temple, a sister temple near Petaling Street.

Rainforest Tours

At about 150 million years old, Malaysia's rainforests are among the world's oldest. They are also among the most diverse in species, with hundreds of thousands of flora and fauna identified and an unknown number still to be identified. Unfortunately, balancing environmental conservation and economic development is tricky, although the government is committed to sustainable development. Guided nature tours can give visitors a good understanding of the various rainforest ecosystems. The most common forest type in and around Kuala Lumpur is the dipterocarp forest. Dipterocarps are the most luxuriant of all plant communities, and comprise many timber species. Mangrove and other swamp forests are usually found in the lowlands, whilst the highest parts of highlands are covered with montane forests. Large animals are difficult to sight in a forest, but smaller creatures are plentiful and fascinating. The best times for a jungle trek are in the early morning or late evening when the forest creatures are liveliest. Trekkers should drink lots of water and wear sturdy walking shoes.

FRIM

Tucked away in the hills northwest of Kuala Lumpur is one of the world's oldest forest research centres. The **Forest Research Institute of Malaysia** (FRIM; daily 7am–7pm; charge; www.frim.gov.my) is a showcase of tropical lowland vegetation spread over 600 hectares (1,480 acres). The Information Centre provides full details, as well as maps (daily 9am–4pm, except some public holidays). FRIM's many attractions include six arboretums, including a world renowned dipterocarp arboretum which contains some of the country's oldest and

On the Canopy Walkway

rarest trees. The main loop road brings you to most of them.

There are also four easy-walking nature trails that wind through the forest, ranging from 1–1.5km (½–1 mile). A fifth trail, the Rover Trail, climbs a steep hill and leads to FRIM's star attraction, the **Canopy Walkway** (Tue–Thur and Sat–Sun 9.30am–2.30pm; register and pay at the Information Centre, registration closes at 1pm; book ahead during school holidays.) This 200m (660ft) long rope-and-ladder walkway was built for scientists to study canopy-level flora and fauna, but visitors also get to appreciate it. The walkway is pretty high up – up to 30m (100ft) above the forest floor – and there are platforms along the way to take a breather and enjoy the view.

Genting Highlands

Large, loud and kitschy define **Genting Highlands** (www.genting.com.my), the Las Vegas of Malaysia. Located an hour's drive northeast of Kuala Lumpur, Genting draws thousands to its hilltop attractions. From the drop-off point halfway up the hill, the spectacular 3.4km (2-mile) **Skyway Cable Car** glides silently above a carpet of montane vegetation (Mon–Thur 7.30am–11pm, Fri–Sun 7.30am–midnight; closed periodically for maintenance).

The ride ends at Genting Hotel, one of seven hotels and apartments here. Follow the signs to get to the theme parks, two of which are indoors and a third outdoors. The Genting Hotel is also the location of Malaysia's only legal casino (24 hours; age limit 21; dress code applies). In addition, three theatres feature local and international cabaret dinner shows, musicals and concerts.

A modern temple looks out over the Genting Highlands

Kuala Gandah Elephant Conservation Centre

With the shrinking of natural forest cover, only 800–1,000 wild elephants are left in Peninsular Malaysia. Animals are increasingly feeding off crops, and being chased off by planters. Individuals that cannot keep up with the herd, including babies and juveniles, are abandoned. As a result, the Department of Wildlife and National Parks set up the **Kuala Gandah National Elephant Conservation Centre** (Sun–Thur 8am–1pm, 2.30–5pm, Fri 8am–12.30pm, 2.45–5pm; donations) as a temporary base for elephants which need to be moved to protected areas or zoos. The centre is in Lanchang, 120km (75 miles) east of Kuala Lumpur.

Riding an elephant

Realising that education and awareness are key to conservation, the Department has been running a visitor programme at the centre, where humans get to interact with six trained elephants. The set programme, which begins at 2pm, allows visitors to feed, ride and bathe elephants. Bring a change of clothes if you intend to get into the river with the elephants. Rides are limited to 120 people per day.

Fraser's Hill

A real contrast to Genting Highlands is **Fraser's Hill**, a peaceful hill resort whose attractions are its cool air and breathtaking mist-shrouded montane forest landscapes. Fraser's Hill is located 104km (65 miles) north of Kuala Lumpur; the jump-off is the whitewater-rafting centre of Kuala Kubu Bharu.

British Malaya's first hill station, the resort is named after an eccentric Englishman who ran a mule transport system and a gambling den for miners and planters. Many of the original 1900s greystone bungalows still stand. The town centre still has the original post office, police station and medical dispensary, but the landmark clock tower is actually a later addition. Check in at the Information Centre (Sun–Fri 8am–9pm, Sat 9am–10pm) for a free map and to book guided nature walks. The ring road around the golf course provides a pleasant two-hour stroll past old bungalows and newer resorts.

Visitors can take a refreshing dip in the **Jeriau waterfall**; note that the steps down are slippery after rain. With some of the richest bird life in the peninsula, Fraser's Hill is a popular birdwatching destination. Nature-lovers should also explore the resort's eight jungle trails, but check trail conditions beforehand at the Information Centre. Break for Devonshire cream tea in the lovely garden of the colonial **Smokehouse Hotel and Restaurant** (daily 3–6pm).

Deep in the Fraser's Hill forest

Kuala Selangor

Standing at the estuary of the Selangor river, 67km (42 miles) from Kuala Lumpur, **Kuala Selangor** was once a great capital whose historical past is partially preserved at **Bukit Melawati**. On this hill is a fort where many bloody battles were fought between the local sultans and the Dutch between 1778 and 1826. A 1.5km (¾-mile) road brings you to the Dutch-built **Altingsburg Lighthouse** (closed to visitors), opposite which is a **lookout** with views of the lush Kuala Selangor Nature Park. Peering over the lookout are six cannons from various periods of the war. Further along the walk are the remains of the **Melawati Gate**, the former gateway to the fort. Close by is the **Royal Burial Ground**

Kuala Selangor Nature Park is popular with birdwatchers

of the first three sultans of Selangor and their families. Entry to the mausoleum is restricted, but visible through the gates is the sacred yellow cloth-covered cannon called the *Penggawa*, the Sultan's most trusted protector.

At the foot of the hill, a road leads to fascinating mangrove forests of the **Kuala Selangor Nature Park** (Taman Alam Kuala Selangor), home to thousands of migratory waterbirds. Register at the Visitors' Centre (daily 8am–6pm; charge), where you will be briefed and receive a leaflet. There are three trails of varying lengths; of note is the brackish lake at the end of the Egret Trail where hundreds of herons congregate and breed.

When darkness descends, **Kampung Kuantan**'s magical firefly display comes on. Between 8 and 10.30pm, local villagers row visitors (RM40 per four passengers per boat) past mangrove trees where millions of tiny male beetles flash synchronously; the flashing rate of three times a minute supposedly makes these the world's brightest fireflies.

WHAT TO DO

SHOPPING

While Kuala Lumpur is not in the same league as the shopping meccas of Singapore and Hong Kong, it does offer variety, quality and bargains. From international brands to Malaysian labels and handcrafted ethnic products, KL has something for every budget. What's more, with the increase in KL-ites' disposable income, 'masstige' brands – prestigious brands at affordable prices – are entering the market. The best bargains are during the annual nationwide Malaysia Mega Sale Carnival, now three months long, with prices slashed up to 70 percent off. Throughout the year, sales are also held by department stores. Sale periods can be crowded, so go early. Traffic can also be exceptionally bad, so use public transport.

Shopping Malls

Shopping malls have become regular hang-outs for KL-ites, and the city just keeps building them, each one bigger than the last. Air-conditioned, they offer consumers not just shops but eateries, cinemas, exhibitions and even ice-skating rinks. Malls are anchored by department stores and supermarkets as well as food courts, and goods for sale usually include household items, books, music, computers and audio-visual equipment. Photography and electronic goods are good buys.

The department stores and boutiques are the best places to buy well-made and affordable tropical-weather **clothes** and **shoes**, although very large sizes might be difficult to get. Among the home-grown labels are consumer brands Padini, Seed and Vincci, and the more upmarket British India and

Brightly coloured kites on sale in Central Market

A traditional kebaya

Loewe; couturiers Zang Toi and Bernard Chandran have an international reputation.

During the major festivals of Chinese New Year, Hari Raya and Deepavali, there is an even greater variety of ethnic or ethnic-inspired clothing and accessories.

The main mall strip is at **Bukit Bintang** *(see page 66)*, while **KLCC** has the high-end Suria KLCC and Avenue K. The **Mid-Valley** city near Brickfields houses the massive Mid-Valley Megamall and its upmarket sister, The Gardens. North of this, in the classy suburb of Bangsar, are the luxury Bangsar Village I & II and the Bangsar Shopping Centre. Petaling Jaya is home to the Sunway Pyramid as well as 1 Utama and The Curve.

Specialist Shops

Move away from the malls and you will discover the cultural side of KL's shopping landscape.

Traditional fabrics are plentiful and both traditional designs and modern variations are available. The ever-popular **batik** is available in a range of fabrics ranging from cotton and voile to silk and satin. Batik fashion has improved by leaps and bounds with government incentives, so well-designed clothes are available now as well as the usual sarongs, accessories, household and decorative items. **Songket**, the hand-woven fabric with intricate tapestry inlaid with gold and metallic threads, appears in formal and ceremonial attire. It is also used as a handbag and shoe covering. From the Bornean state of Sarawak, woven **pua kumbu** textiles feature beautiful indigenous designs. Shop for these fabrics at Central Market and the Kuala Lumpur Craft Centre. Jalan Masjid India and Jalan Tuanku Abdul Rahman are great for *songket* and batik. For textiles, head to the wholesale quarter of Jalan Tuanku Abdul Rahman, where you can also buy traditional Malay, Chinese and Indian outfits.

Gold jewellery is affordable and comes in contemporary or Malay-, Chinese- or Indian-influenced designs. Local gold-smiths use pure gold (up to 24-carat). Bargains can be found along Jalan Masjid India and Jalan Tuanku Abdul Rahman. **Kelantan silver** is fashioned into a variety of items, from brooches and costume jewellery to serving dishes and table-ware, and is available in Central Market and the Kuala Lumpur Craft Centre. Malaysia's **pewterware** is renowned internationally for its stylish handmade designs. These can be found in malls and the Royal Selangor Pewter factory.

Malaysian and Asian **handicrafts** include bamboo and rattan products, traditional kites *(wau)*, pottery and Bornean beadwork. Shop for these at the Kuala Lumpur Craft Centre, Suria KLCC, Central Market and Peter Hoe.

The Art of Bargaining

Prices are fixed in shopping malls and chain stores, but elsewhere, customers are expected to bargain. It is a bit of an act, but bargaining is also a great way to interact with locals. Being the first or last customer of the day usually gets you a good price, as does paying cash.

When you bargain, shop around so you know what the price range is. Especially in tourist areas, start by knocking 50 percent (or more) off the price, then increase the amount you are prepared to pay as the salesperson reduces their price. If you are not prepared to pay their 'final price', walk away; if your offer is within their profit range, they will call you back. If they do not, you know you have gone too low.

Night markets

Pasar malam or night markets are a great opportunity to experience local colour. Stalls are set up at around 6pm, and locals come to buy everything from fresh produce to underwear. Check out the *pasar malam* along Jalan Masjid India (Sat), Jalan Berhala in Brickfields (Thur) and Jalan Telawi Satu in Bangsar (Sun). The most famous *pasar malam* is the Petaling Street Bazaar (see pages 33–4).

Markets and Galleries

Cheap goods like T-shirts, jeans, leather products, and art and curios can be purchased at street markets like the **Petaling Street Bazaar** (which specialises in fake branded items) and the **Jalan Haji Taib** market near Kampung Baru. Petaling Street is also the wholesale centre of women's accessories. The Saturday-night **Laman Santai** at the National Art Gallery serves up more handicrafts and artwork.

The many different media and styles that make up Malaysian contemporary art make it a great souvenir and a good investment to boot. Tourist-targeted commercial artwork can be bought at the **Annexe**, Central Market, while more expensive pieces by established and up-and-coming artists are available in art galleries throughout the city. For a list of galleries and exhibitions go to Kakiseni (www.kakiseni.com).

ENTERTAINMENT

Kuala Lumpur has one of the hottest clubbing scenes in the region, with a plethora of venues ranging from warehouses to exclusive clubs, where international and local DJs spin a wide spectrum of dance and other music, as well as live acts that feature commercial and more eclectic material. Watering holes are also plentiful, and wine-drinking has firmly set in. The arts scene is smaller but active and reflects both historical Asian as well as modern Western influences in music, dance, theatre and visual arts. For information on what's happening where, check newspapers as well as magazines like *Faces* (www.faces.com), *Juice* (www.juiceonline.com) and *Time Out* (www.timeoutkl.com). For discerning write-ups and listings, go to Kakiseni (www.kakiseni.com).

Nightlife

Friday and Saturday nights are the best times to party in KL. KL-ites come out in full force, dressed up and ready to have fun. The action starts late, at around 11pm, and goes on until 2–3am. After this, do not be surprised to see clubbers head for supper! Live bands start their gigs at around 10pm. Clubs charge an entry fee from 10 or 11pm, which includes one drink. A good range of alcohol is stocked, but drinks are expensive, so do take advantage of happy hour, usually 5.30–9pm, when drinks are half-price; and ladies' nights, Wednesdays in most places, which offer free drinks for women. Beers start at RM10 a glass and RM40 a jug, spirits at RM15, and wine at RM25 a glass and RM80 a bottle. You can keep a tab going until you leave. Waiters generally expect a tip.

Cocktails at Frangipani

KL-ites tend to dress up to go to the fancier clubs, and some places do enforce dress codes which for men stipulate, at the minimum, a collared T-shirt, long trousers and covered shoes; other places have a no jeans, shorts and sandals rule. Most clubs adhere to the 21-year-old age limit (the legal drinking age) and in clubs patronised mainly by Muslims little alcohol is consumed.

Clubs are gay-friendly and nightlife choices for the gay community abound, although they are not openly advertised because of secular and religious laws.

Clubs

Head for the entertainment clusters, which feature multi-outlet complexes comprising at least one club, a chill-out bar and a restaurant. **Jalan P Ramlee** near the KLCC features giants like Espanda, Nouvo, The Beach Club Café, Grand Modesto's, Rum Jungle and Poppy Collection. Nearby on Jalan Ampang is the ultra-hip **Zouk Club**. Where swanky is concerned, the Jalan Doraisamy area continues to reign with **Maison and Bed** and **Asian Heritage Row** establishments like The Loft, Atrium and Bar Club. Changkat Bukit Bintang's gems are the gay club **Frangipani** and **Little Havana**. Most good hotels have clubs as standard fixtures; notable outfits are Kuala Lumpur Hilton's exclusive **Zeta Bar**, The Westin's sizzling **Qba** and the old favourite, **Baze** at the Renaissance.

The ultra-hip Zouk Club

Live Music

Live jazz has made a comeback, so great acts are performing in Jalan Doraisamy at **Mezza Notte** (Asian Heritage Row); Bukit Bintang at **Bangkok Jazz** (Chulan Square), **Yoko's** (Changkat Bukit Bintang) and **No Black Tie** (Jalan Mesui); and Jalan Ampang at **Alexis Bistro Ampang** (Great Eastern Mall). Alexis and No Black Tie are also among the best places to catch gigs by local musicians and songwriters.

Live music at No Black Tie

Mainstream bands perform regularly at **Planet Hollywood** (KL Plaza) and **Hard Rock Café** (Concorde Hotel), while popular venues for underground music are the **Annexe** (Central Market) and **MCPA Hall** (Chinese Assembly Hall). Hotel lounges usually feature good Filipino bands playing covers.

Pubs and Bars

Good hotels have lounges or bars where you can wind down with a drink, and these vary from traditional English outfits like The Pub at Shangri-la to Luna Bar at the Pacific Regency Hotel Suites, with its breathtaking views, and the first-of-its-kind Champagne Lounge at the Grand Millennium.

Like clubs, watering holes are clustered in the entertainment areas. Bintang Walk features Starhill Gallery's trendy Feast Floor choices; Changkat Bukit Bintang has charming little pubs in pre-war shophouses; Suria KLCC has its esplanade-facing outlets, while for glamour, Jalan Doraisamy has its Asian Heritage Row hang-outs. Outside the city centre,

Traditional dance at the Citawarna Festival

the once-trendy Bangsar has lost some of its lustre but is still worth checking out, while other favourite chill-out places are the Petaling Jaya enclaves of Sri Hartamas and The Curve.

The Arts

Traditional Malay performances of dance, music and theatre have been relegated to mainly tourist events, with the only regular showcases being at the Malaysia Tourism Centre and the National Art Gallery's Laman Santai. However, you can catch performances from time to time at the Experimental Theatre, Petronas Philharmonic Hall and Kuala Lumpur Performing Arts Centre (KLPAC).

However, the **classical Indian dance** movement is very active. The key exponents are the Sutra Dance Theatre and the Temple of Fine Arts, and performances are staged at KLPAC and Sutra House. **Traditional Chinese performances** are not staged regularly, although Chinese orchestra Dama is one name to look out for. Chinese opera is only performed during the Hungry Ghost Festival.

Contemporary performances of theatre and dance are staged regularly and draw from both Western and local traditions. Venues for these are KLPAC, the Annexe Central Market, The Actors Studio Bangsar and Istana Budaya.

The **Petronas Philharmonic Hall** has a good year-long classical music performance programme. Regional and foreign acts sometimes feature in these venues.

For **visual arts**, galleries are opening all the time, including alternative art spaces. Check out local artists' work at venues like the National Art Gallery, Petronas Art Gallery, Islamic Arts Museum, Valentine Willie Fine Art, Gallery Taksu, Wei-Ling Gallery and NN Gallery.

Cinemas

Despite the wide availability of DVDs, KL's cinemas attract a steady clientele. Local cinemas are state-of-the-art, air-conditioned and cheap, with some chains offering THX sound and luxury halls. Choose from mainstream Hollywood, Bollywood and Hong Kong fare, with a scattering of local Malay-language films, Southeast Asian movies and arthouse releases. Blockbusters often get released on the same day as in the US, UK or Hong Kong, and queues can be long.

Non-Malay-language movies have Bahasa Malaysia and Mandarin subtitles, and censorship can sometimes be irritating. Multi-hall cinemas are operated by either Golden Screen Cinema or Tanjung Golden Village. The former also operates an IMAX Theatre in Berjaya Times Square.

Independent Films

Malaysia is experiencing a renaissance in independent film-making. Thanks to digital video, Malaysian film-makers have been carving an international reputation for producing award-winning short films. Established names to look out for are Amir Muhammad, James Lee, Ho Yuhang and Tan Chui Mui. Meanwhile, Yasmin Ahmad produces ground-breaking feature-length films that cross ethnic boundaries through love stories.

Check listings for short film and indie festivals, usually held at the Annexe (Central Market), PalatePalette Restaurant (Jalan Mesui), Help Institute (Petaling Jaya) and the Kuala Lumpur Performing Arts Centre (Sentul).

SPORTS

Spectator Sports

Malaysians are mad about **football**, which they call *bola*, whether it's the English Premier League or the Malaysia Cup. Fans dress up in club colours and get quite excited during live matches, whether at stadia or live telecasts at pubs and 24-hour *mamak* centres. **Formula One** fans flock to the Sepang International Circuit each year to watch motorsport's premier race and party in the city. The annual **KL International Tower Jump** draws crowds as BASE jumpers defy death from the top of the KL Tower, using parachutes that open at low airspeeds.

Canoeing on Sungai Selangor

Participant Sports

Hotels with a four-star rating and above have swimming pools and gym facilities or fitness centres; often these offer yoga, aerobics or pilates classes as well. There are special sprung **jogging trails** at the Lake Gardens and KLCC Park. The Titiwangsa Lake Gardens behind the National Art Gallery also has jogging and walking trails. Runners should also contact the Kuala Lumpur Hash House Harriers (www.motherhash.org), a running and beer-drinking group with roots in colonial times, which conducts family-oriented fun runs all over the city and its surrounds.

Good hotels should be able to arrange **golf** sessions. KL is surrounded by good golf courses, with at least 50 within an hour's drive of the city. Some are beautifully and professionally designed, and others offer night golfing under floodlights. Visitors have to pay green fees (RM80–400) and produce handicap cards. For details, contact the Malaysian Golfing Association (www.mga online.com.my).

Spas

Although it had been lagging behind its neighbours, Malaysia has hopped firmly onto the spa bandwagon. KL now features international spa chains, beautifully designed venues, and attractive packages for different budgets. Choose from hour-long treatments to vacation spas in hotels that combine a wide variety of recreational activities with treatments.

Bowling enthusiasts will appreciate the facilities and long opening hours at the state-of-the-art 38-lane Cosmic Bowl (Mid-Valley Megamall) and 48-lane Pyramid Megalanes (Sunway Pyramid), where the national bowling team trains.

Nature-Based Sports

Many of the places listed in the Day Trips section *(see pages 74–81)* offer opportunities to try adventure sports. **Jungle trekking** is the best way to experience the natural beauty of the country. Always check in first with information centres or park authorities, dress adequately, carry enough water and bring insect repellent. **Whitewater sports** are popular in Kuala Kubu Bharu, the jump-off for Fraser's Hill. Have a go at rafting, canoeing or tubing (floating down a stream on a rubber tube). For **caving**, guided nature tours of a limestone cave ecosystem is conducted at the Dark Caves, a passage in Batu Caves. Choose from a 20-minute or hour-long nature tour or get down and dirty in the three- to four-hour-long adventure caving tour. For licensed operators, *see page 116.*

CHILDREN'S KUALA LUMPUR

Kuala Lumpur has fun activities for children of all ages, although it is not very baby-friendly, as facilities for breastfeeding and nappy-changing, as well as pushchairs, are inadequate.

The best children's activity in town is the interactive science discovery centre **Petrosains** *(see page 60)*, at Suria KLCC, whose innovative displays provide hours of fun and learning. Also at KLCC, the **Petronas Philharmonic Hall** holds family fun days. **The Actors Studio** (www.theactorsstudio.com.my) stages children's theatre performances from time to time.

The **School of Hard Knocks**, at the Royal Selangor Pewter Factory in Setapak Jaya (http://visitorcentre.royalselangor.com; bookings compulsory), offers children the chance to create their own pewter masterpieces with a few simple tools. Batik, pottery and woodcraft workshops are held at the **Kuala Lumpur Craft Complex** *(see page 70)* and the Saturday-night **Laman Santai** in the National Art Gallery car park *(see page 50)*.

The **Sunway Lagoon Water Theme Park** *(see page 75)* has great rides, plus the world's largest man-made surf beach and longest pedestrian suspension bridge. There are large children's playgrounds at the **KLCC Park** and the **Lake Gardens**. The former also has a wading pool. The latter offers a host of wildlife experiences at the Bird Park, Butterfly Park and Deer Park. The ultimate animal experience is at **Kuala Gandah Elephant Conservation Centre**, where children can interact with Asian Elephants, as well as learning about conservation.

A carousel ride

Calendar of Events

Many festival dates are not fixed as they follow the lunar and Muslim calendars. Check exact dates with Tourism Malaysia (www.tourism.gov.my).

January/February: *Thaipusam*, the festival of repentance, celebrated by Hindus bearing milkpots and *kavadi* structures at the holy shrine of Batu Caves; *Federal Territory Day* (1 Feb): parades and other events in celebration of Kuala Lumpur's birthday; *Chinese New Year*: the start of the lunar year is celebrated with festive goodies and decorations.

March: *National Craft Day*: week-long festival of handicrafts from all over Malaysia at the Kuala Lumpur Craft Complex; *Malaysian Formula One Grand Prix*: Formula One action at the Sepang International Circuit.

May: *Wesak Day*: devotees offer prayers and give alms to monks in Buddhist temples to commemorate Buddha's birth, enlightenment and death; *Colours of Malaysia (Citrawarna)*: a colourful festival showcasing Malaysia's cultural diversity, kicked off by an extravagant parade along Jalan Raja; *Malaysia Mega Sale Carnival* (May–Aug): huge country-wide sale.

July/August: *National Day* (31 Aug): Independence Day is marked with parades and concerts, beginning on the eve with a countdown in Dataran Merdeka.

September: *Festival of the Hungry Ghosts*: Chinese street operas and concerts staged to appease the spirits of the dead; *Mooncake Festival*: this mid-Autumn festival is celebrated with mooncakes and colourful lanterns.

October/November: *Deepavali*: the Hindu Festival of Lights is marked by prayers and celebrations – Brickfields is particularly exciting.

December: *Christmas* (25 Dec): festive decor and carolling in malls, and midnight church masses; *New Year's Eve* (31 Dec): concerts, countdowns and fireworks in Bukit Bintang and KLCC.

Variable dates: *Hari Raya Puasa*: the city is painted green as Muslims usher in the end of the Ramadhan fasting month with prayers, feasts and visits to friends and family; during Ramadan, special bazaars spring up all over the city; *Hari Raya Haji*: this Muslim festival marking the *haj* (pilgrimage to Mecca) is observed mainly with prayers.

EATING OUT

From the fragrant brown cinnamon bark to the sour pulp of the tamarind, the spicy flower buds of cloves to the pungent rhizome of the galangal, it was the spices of the Malay lands that spurred trade, fuelled the rise and fall of empires, and influenced the world's gastronomy. These aromatic products attracted a host of peoples to the Malay peninsula, who, in turn, brought ingredients, cooking styles and food from their own lands. At the same time, the mixing of these peoples through the ages encouraged the hybridisation and enriching of local tastes, textures and flavour. The result is modern Malaysian food, astonishing in its variety and uniqueness.

Kuala Lumpur is a culinary microcosm of the country, because when Malaysians from all over the country settled in the city, they brought their cuisines with them. Hence, the regional Peninsula specialities are all available, from the sour and spicy northern dishes to the creamy curries of the south and the fish specialities of the east coast. With increased income and globalisation, KL-ites have also developed sophisticated palates, evident in the host of chic bistros and fine-dining restaurants offering Asian and Continental fare.

Smoking allowed

Although smoking is officially not allowed in enclosed restaurants, the rule is ignored in *mamak* outfits almost all the time, and in some bistros and cafes, with 'smoking' tables placed near the entrance.

Innovations abound, from entire cuisines such as Nyonya food to Chinese style stir-fried vegetables served with Indian curries. Nonetheless, it is hawker food that reigns, simple wholesome fare from age-old recipes dished up in no-frills coffee shops and roadside stalls.

The plenitude of eating places is due to Malaysians' great fondness for eating out. Because it is affordable and convenient, eating out daily for lunch and even dinner is normal. An evening out almost always starts with food, and often ends with it, too. Hawker stalls and 24-hour *mamak* (Indian-Muslim) joints allow KL-ites to enjoy a light Indian *roti* snack or steaming-hot Chinese noodles at any time.

Outlets can be crowded at weekends and festive holidays, especially child-friendly eateries and new restaurants. KL-ites will also travel great distances to sample the best,

Eating out on Petaling Street

even driving to another town. Ambience and cleanliness do not really matter – it is the taste that counts.

Below are the main cuisines found in KL described in broad strokes and a few staples. The main meal across all local cuisines comprises white rice served with several meat and vegetable dishes which are shared communally.

Malay Cuisine

The fresh, aromatic spices of the land, combined with herbs from India, the Middle East and China, are what define the spicy and robust flavours of Malay food. The cuisine traditionally features rice, fish, fresh vegetables and the chilli-based *sambal*, often made with *belacan* (shrimp paste). Food is always seasoned with spices, and coconut milk and the sour tamarind juice are important ingredients.

The day for many Malaysians usually starts with *nasi lemak*, rice cooked in coconut milk served with condiments like peanuts, fried anchovies, cucumber, egg and a *sambal*. Another popular dish is satay, marinated and charcoal-grilled skewered chicken, beef or mutton; it is served with a thick, spicy peanut sauce. Common dishes that accompany rice are *ayam masak merah*, a piquant chicken dish cooked with tomatoes and chillies; *rendang*, a dry beef or chicken curry; and *ikan bakar*, fish wrapped in a banana leaf and charcoal-grilled. Salads are also popular, eaten raw *(ulam)* or in a spicy mix *(kerabu)*. Malay food also includes a large variety of *kuih* (cakes) featuring coconut, glutinous rice, bananas or palm sugar.

Regional innovations and peculiarities are evident in dishes such as beef cooked in the *rendang tok* style, with slices of young coconut in it, and *ayam percik*, grilled chicken coated

Fusion Fare

The word in trendy dining amongst KL's chi-chi set is fusion fare, generally a mix of Eastern and Western ingredients and cooking styles. However, with so much good traditional food available – and the organic evolution of the traditional Nyonya and Eurasian fusion cuisines – purists tend to dismiss contemporary fusion fare as faddish, presentation-focused or an excuse for exorbitant pricing in the name of novelty.

The counter-argument to this is that because there *is* so much good traditional food, local and international chefs have a huge palette with which to experiment. Today, all sorts of fusion fare are available, from the El Bulli-influenced molecular gastronomy of Lafitte in the Shangri-la Hotel to the *sosaku* creative Japanese cuisine of Hotel Maya's Still Waters restaurant, and in Suria KLCC, Aseana Café's innovative takes on Asian dishes.

with a spicy coconut sauce. Food from the east coast tends to be sweeter and richer, while that from the south has Arabic influences.

Where to go: The best Malay food is in Kampung Baru, where stalls and *kampung* (village)-style eateries dominate. Festive specialities abound during the Muslim fasting month of Ramadan.

Satay – a Malaysian classic

Chinese Cuisine

Most Malaysian Chinese cuisine comprises the southern regional styles of China, from where early migrants originated. Food is stir-fried, steamed or deep-fried, and meat dishes, soups and noodles are occasionally infused with local elements like black pepper, curry leaves and *sambal*.

A quintessentially KL dish is the hawker preparation of Hokkien *mee*, thick yellow wheat noodles fried in dark soy sauce with pork and prawns. Another Hokkien favourite is *bak kut teh*, a fragrant herbal soup of pork ribs. From the Cantonese come such favourites as *char siu* (barbecued pork) and refined multi-course banquets. *Dim sum* is a feast in itself, with numerous varieties of steamed, fried or baked dumplings and more.

Many Hainanese immigrants operate *kopitiam* or coffee shops, which serve the perennial favourite, Hainanese chicken rice, as well as noodles and good tea and coffee. They were also favoured as cooks for the colonials, resulting in Chinese variations of chicken chop and pork chop. Teochew porridge is a popular supper option, where plain rice broth is eaten with salty, preserved food, as well as richer fare like braised goose. The Hakkas originated *yong tau fu*, an assortment of bean curd and vegetables stuffed with fish and meat paste.

Chinese hawker fare from the northern Malaysian state of Penang is the most famous and, some argue, the tastiest; must-tries include *char kway teow*, stir-fried flat noodles with prawns and bean-sprouts, and Hokkien *mee* or prawn *mee* (not to be confused with the KL Hokkien *mee*), featuring noodles in a light, spicy pork-flavoured soup.

Where to go: Check out the Chinese fare in Bukit Bintang and Petaling Street, but good restaurants, hawker centres and *kopitiam* are found all over KL.

Indian Cuisine
Because of its dominance in the culinary landscape, piquant Tamil cuisine, typified by breads and 'banana leaf rice' meals,

Preparing 'banana leaf rice'

has become synonymous with 'Indian food' in Malaysia. The former comprises griddled breads like *roti canai* and *thosai* accompanied by the lentil *dhal* dish or a curry. Like the Malay *nasi lemak*, *roti canai* has become a favourite breakfast dish of all Malaysians.

Ordering 'banana leaf rice' will see a banana leaf placed before you on which hot rice is heaped along with three different vegetables and a choice of chicken or beef cur-

Delicious Indian sweets

rics – usually a dry *varuval* or coconut-milk-laced curry – or fried fish. These eateries also serve good vegetarian meals.

In the last five years or so, 24-hour Indian Muslim or *mamak* eateries have proliferated, serving delicious *halal* South Indian food. These have roots in Penang's *nasi kandar*, named after the way early Indian Muslim hawkers used to carry rice *(nasi)* and curry in two baskets balanced on a *kandar*, or pole. Traditional *nasi kandar* curries include fish-head curry and tiger prawn masala. Some of these *mamak* serve the North Indian tandoori favourites and *biryani* rice, too.

North Indian restaurants are higher-end, and KL-ites tend to gravitate towards the tandoori and *naan* bread sets, although a wide variety of food is available. Certainly, the finer dishes of the maharajahs are available in sumptuously appointed restaurants, completed with live music.

Where to go: Brickfields and Jalan Masjid India have the range of Indian eateries, while every row of shops anywhere in KL will have at least one *mamak* shop.

Nyonya Cuisine

A delicious hybrid of Malay and Chinese cuisines that evolved over centuries, Nyonya food, also called Peranakan or Straits Chinese food, is largely flavoured by well-blended, complex spice pastes. The cuisine took root in the 15th century when traders from China started settling down in the Malay peninsula, marrying locals and adopting local customs.

A lovely starter is *pai ti* (also known as top hats), a savoury bean, shrimp or pork and carrot mixture served in a delicate pastry shell. Dishes like *kari kapitan*, a coconut-based chicken curry, *lemak nenas* (pineapple curry) and *buah keluak kay* (chicken braised with mangrove nuts) are more Malay in character, while dishes like *loh bak* (meat rolls) and *hong bak* (pork braised in spices and bean paste) are decidedly more Chinese. No Nyonya meal is complete without *sambal belacan* (chili and dried shrimp paste) and a dash of lime.

Classy snacking in the Peter Hoe Beyond café

Laksa, a soupy noodle dish, comes in two versions: curry *laksa* has a rich red gravy with a coconut milk base, while *asam laksa* has a fish-based sour, tangy soup.

Like the Malays, the Nyonyas are also famous for their painstakingly prepared desserts, such as *pulut tai tai* (sticky blue-and-white rice cakes) served with *kaya* (coconut egg jam) and the Chinese New Year speciality of *kuih kapek*, crispy folded biscuits.

Where to go: Good Nyonya restaurants are hard to find; downtown, Precious Old China in Central Market and its sister restaurant, Old China Café near Petaling Street, have cornered the market.

Other Cuisines

While cuisines from the rest of the world have long been part of KL's dining scene, they have assumed a wider and more sophisticated flavour recently. Continental, Mediterranean, Mexican and Middle Eastern restaurants have become part of local choices, as have Japanese, Korean, Thai and Indochinese ones. Besides the downtown entertainment clusters, many eateries are located near embassies or expatriate enclaves in the upmarket sections of Jalan Ampang and Bangsar.

Drinks

Tea and coffee are copiously drunk in KL, and a range of preparations is available, so be specific when ordering. Among local favourites is *teh tarik*. Made of tea powder, condensed milk and evaporated milk, this 'pulled tea' is prepared by repeatedly pouring it from a glass held high into another

held below. This creates a thick froth, cools down the tea and ensures a thorough mix. This art can be witnessed in coffee shops, but there are even national-level *teh tarik*-making competitions! American coffee-shop chains such as Starbucks and San Francisco are plentiful and popular. Chinese tea is drunk with Chinese food, although in *kopitiam* herbal variations are popular, too.

KL-ites sometimes just order a glass of warm water to go with their meal; this is generally boiled water from the tap, but mineral water is also available. Ice cubes are safe to have in large restaur-

High tea at the Carcosa Hotel

ants, but tourists should avoid those made from tap water. Sugar is usually added to freshly squeezed fruit juices, and juices advertised as fresh sometimes come out of bottles.

Muslims are not permitted by their religion to drink alcohol, and it is therefore generally not available in Muslim eateries. However, elsewhere alcohol can easily be ordered, with beer and stout being the most popular, even in Chinese *kopitiam*. Wines are also popular, especially table wines and New World varieties, but a wide range and high-quality labels are now available in the restaurants, clubs and wine and cigar bars patronised by discerning KL-ites. However, alcohol is extremely expensive, so KL-ites take full advantage of happy hour two-for-the-price-of-one deals.

To Help You Order…

You can use English to order your food in restaurants, but Bahasa Malaysia is useful at hawker stalls and *mamak* shops.

Do you have…?	**Ada tak… ?**
I'd like this/that.	**Saya mahu ini/itu.**
I don't want this/that.	**Saya tidak mahu ini/itu.**
I eat only vegetarian food.	**Saya hanya makan makanan sayuran.**
I can eat spicy food.	**Saya boleh makan makanan pedas.**
Not spicy.	**Tidak pedas.**
The bill, please.	**Tolong beri saya bil.**

a little	**sedikit**	cup	**cawan**
a lot	**banyak**	bowl	**mangkuk**
delicious	**sedap**	fork	**garpu**
sour	**masam**	spoon	**sudu**
sweet	**manis**	glass	**gelas**
bread	**roti**	beef	**daging**
fruit	**buah**	fish	**ikan**
egg noodles	**mee**	pork	**babi**
vermicelli	**meehoon**	soup	**sup**
flat noodles	**kway teow**	vegetables	**sayur**
ice	**ais**	rice	**nasi**

coffee with/without milk	**kopi/kopi o**
iced coffee	**kopi ais**
tea with/without milk	**teh/teh o**
Chinese tea	**teh Cina**
iced lime juice	**limau ais**
sugarcane juice	**air tebu**
beer	**bir**
iced water	**ais kosong**

HANDY TRAVEL TIPS

An A–Z Summary of Practical Information

A

ACCOMMODATION

Some of Asia's best hotels in every price range can be found in Kuala Lumpur, with the continued glut of rooms ensuring that quality accommodation is affordable. Luxury hotels are extremely reasonable, and good budget accommodation is also available, usually housed in pre-war shophouses and offering requisite internet facilities, air conditioning, laundry and lockers.

The big luxury hotel chains are all here, most located in the Golden Triangle, with views of the Petronas Twin Towers and/or Kuala Lumpur Tower offered as selling points. Bukit Bintang has a range of accommodation, including some interesting three-star boutique hotels. The more established backpacker hostels are in the old city centre areas of Petaling Street and the adjacent Puduraya near the main bus station. Behind Jalan Bukit Bintang, Tengkat Tong Shin and surrounds host the new breed of funky 'flash packing' budget offerings.

Published rates usually include 10 percent service and 5 percent government tax, and most include a buffet breakfast. Actual rates are often lower, and discounts can be negotiated for longer stays. Hotels that target business travellers usually offer discounts at weekends. Internet rates are lower than walk-in or call-in rates.

A surcharge is usually imposed for peak periods: long weekends, Malaysian and Singaporean school holidays and public holidays, particularly Hari Raya Puasa and Chinese New Year, the Formula One Grand Prix period, and the peak Arab tourist months of July and August, when advance bookings are strongly advised.

AIRPORTS

There are two airports that service international flights. Feeder buses running at 20-minute intervals link the two terminals.

KLIA. Over 50 airlines land in the Kuala Lumpur International Airport (KLIA; tel: 03-8776 4386; www.klia.com.my), a large and modern airport located 70km (43 miles) south of KL. Planes arrive and depart from four satellite arms which are linked to the main terminal building via an aerotrain (3–5-minute intervals).

From KLIA, the fastest way to the city centre is by the high-speed KLIA Ekspres Train, also known as the ERL (5am–midnight, 20-minute intervals; www.kliaekspres.com; RM35) which takes 28 minutes to reach the KL Sentral Station; from there, taxis, inter-city trains and buses are plentiful. Airport Limo takes 40–60 minutes to reach your destination in the city. Buy a coupon at the airport (RM67 budget, RM92 premier; midnight–6am surcharge). Airport Coach takes over an hour to reach town, departing from the airport basement (6.15am–12.30am, 30-minute intervals; RM20) to Hentian Duta, slightly out of town, but it makes drop-offs at major hotels.

For departures, you can take the KLIA Ekspres Train, Airport Limo (tel: 03-9223 8080, 8am–midnight, or tel: 03-8787 3030, midnight–8am) or any taxi (surcharge plus meter).

LCC-T. Budget airlines are serviced by the Low Cost Carrier Terminal (LCC-T; tel: 03-8777 8888; www.klia.com.my/lccterminal), which is 20km (12 miles) from KLIA and takes 10 minutes longer to reach from KL. This is a more basic airport than KLIA, but it still has eateries and money-exchange facilities. Many bus companies go to KL Sentral from the LCC-T, including the Skybus (7am–1.15am, 30-minute intervals; www.skybus.com.my; RM9) and Airport Coach (5am–12.30am, 45-minute intervals; RM20) to Hentian Duta. You can also take coupon LCC-T taxis (RM56 budget, RM92 premier; midnight–6am surcharge).

For departures, you can take the Skybus (tel: 03-9223 8080, 3.30am–11.10pm), LCC-T taxis (tel: 03-8787 4113) or any taxi (surcharge plus meter).

Avoid touts offering 'cheap' taxi rides at both airports – you usually end up paying a lot more. Also note that the Sultan Abdul Aziz Shah or Subang Airport, which services Fokker 50 domestic flights, is located 20km (12 miles) from KL (tel: 03-7836 1833).

B

BUDGETING FOR YOUR TRIP

On average, allow RM200 a day without accommodation, although travelling off-peak and being particularly frugal could cut that down to RM100–150. Below are some indicative costs, with the caveat that inflation in KL is about 3–5 percent per year.

Accommodation for every budget is good value in KL, starting at RM60 for decent budget accommodation, with the newer, fancier outfits being very good value indeed. RM300 will get you a good room in a good three- or four-star hotel. Rates for five-star hotels are a fraction of New York or London prices.

Food is very affordable, with RM30 buying you a good meal with non-alcoholic drinks; street food is extremely cheap, going as low as RM5 for a meal with drinks. Most hotels throw in a free break-fast with the room. Alcohol is very expensive, though, with beer costing RM10–14 a pop, so take advantage of happy hour.

Transport is cheap if you use trains and buses within the city, and RM10 per day should suffice. Taxis charge RM2 for the first kilo-metre (½ mile), with a 10-sen increase every 200m/yds. From mid-night to 6am there is a surcharge of 50 percent on the metered fare. Surcharges also apply for bookings (RM2), baggage placed in the boot (RM1 per piece) and additional passengers beyond two (RM1 each). Car-hire prices start at RM150. Airport transfers are around RM35 by train, RM25 by bus and RM80 by taxi.

Admission fees are generally reasonable for attractions (RM5–20) and theatre performances (RM40–150).

C

CAR HIRE AND DRIVING

Driving within KL is not recommended, as traffic is horrendous and signage confusing. Avoid driving in the city unless you are used to challenging driving conditions and ill-mannered drivers. However, driving outside the city on excursions is a pleasure not to be missed.

Malaysia operates a left-hand driving system and an international driver's licence is required except for tourists from Australia, Japan, the EU, New Zealand, Singapore and the US. Petrol is slightly over RM2 a litre, and stations are plentiful, even along the highways. Note that road signs are in Bahasa Malaysia and can be inadequate, so buy a good, recent KL road map and plan your route.

Major car-rental companies have 24-hour counters at the KLIA, as well as branches in other major cities where you can drop off your car. Rental starts from RM150 for the compact Malaysian-made Proton car and includes insurance and unlimited mileage. Chauffeur-driven cars are also available.

Reputable companies include: **Avis Malaysia**, tel: 03-7628 2300, www.avis.com.my; **Mayflower Car Rental**, tel: 03-6253 1888, www.mayflowercarrental.com; and **Kasina Rent-A-Car**, tel: 03-8787 1739, www.kasina.com.my.

road	**jalan**	north	**utara**
lane	**lorong**	south	**selatan**
street	**lebuh**	east	**timur**
highway	**lebuhraya**	west	**barat**
bridge	**jambatan**	entry	**masuk**
junction	**simpang**	exit	**keluar**
where	**di mana**	turn	**belok**
left	**kiri**	inside	**dalam**
right	**kanan**	outside	**luar**
go	**pergi**	front	**hadapan**
stop	**berhenti**	behind	**belakang**
near	**dekat**		or **depan**
far	**jauh**	here	**sini**
follow	**ikut**	there	**sana**

danger	awas/merbahaya
no overtaking	dilarang memotong
slow down	kurangkan laju
speed limit	had laju
detour	lencongan
keep left/right	ikut kiri/kanan
one-way street	jalan sehala
Can you help me?	Bolehkah cik tolong saya?
Where is this place?	Di mana tempat ini?
How far?	Berapa jauh?
I want to go to...	Saya hendak pergi ke...
Please stop here.	Tolong berhenti di sini.
follow	ikut

CLIMATE

On average, the temperature is 33°C (91°F) during the day, and 24°C (75°F) at night. The hottest months are January to March. Showers and thunderstorms are occasional and usually confined to evenings, and the wettest months are April–May and October–November. Humidity is high at 80 percent. Thick haze from plantation fires during the El Nino years can envelop the city between July and October.

Details on local weather can be found on the Malaysian Meteorological Department homepage: www.met.gov.my/home_e.html.

CLOTHING

Cottons and natural fibres work best in Kuala Lumpur's climate. Shorts and T-shirts are generally acceptable, including in shopping malls, although KL-ites do tend to dress up for a night on the town. If you intend to visit places of worship or travel outside of KL, pack clothing that covers your arms and legs. For footwear, slip-ons are handy, as shoes must be removed before entering temples and homes. If you intend to jungle-trek, pack tougher shoes. Sunglasses and umbrellas or raincoats come in handy.

CRIME AND SAFETY

Purse snatching and petty theft have become quite severe, so make sure your belongings are secure and use waist pouches or backpacks. Snatch thieves tend to comprise two men on a motorcycle or leaning out of moving cars. If your bag is snatched, let go of it, because many thieves carry knives which they will not hesitate to use. When walking along the street, always face oncoming traffic and make sure your bag is on your side that is away from the road. Pickpockets operate in crowded areas like trains and buses.

When sightseeing, only carry what you need, though you are required to have your passport on you. However, police will only ask to see your ID if you have committed a crime or are in a nightspot that is being raided. Never buy anything from touts, whether bus or train tickets or admission tickets to attractions, which are usually free. Report any crime to the nearest police station (tel: 999) or the Tourist Police (tel: 03-2149 6590), who patrol tourist spots. The latter can help with lost passports and other documents as well.

CUSTOMS AND ENTRY REQUIREMENTS

Passports must have minimum six months' validity at the time of entry. Visa requirements change, so before travelling, check with your Malaysian embassy/consulate or the Immigration Department website (www.imi.gov.my). Generally, though, no visa is needed for citizens of Commonwealth countries (with exceptions); the US (unlimited period); most EU countries (up to three months); all Asian countries except Myanmar; and some other EU countries (up to one month). Most tourists can get a visa on arrival at the KLIA for a 30-day social visit pass (RM100).

Prohibited goods include drugs, dangerous chemicals, pornography, firearms and ammunition. Drug possession carries a mandatory death sentence. Upon arrival in Malaysia, declare all taxable goods; for details, check the Customs website at www.customs. gov.my. You may have to pay a deposit for temporary importation, refundable on departure – usually 50 percent of the value. Keep your receipt of purchase and obtain an official receipt for any tax or deposit paid. Among duty-free items are cameras, watches, pens, portable radio-cassette players, perfume, cosmetics and lighters.

E

ELECTRICITY

Electrical outlets are rated at 220 volts, 50 cycles and serve three-pin, flat-pronged plugs. American products do not work here, but most supermarkets stock adaptors. Major hotels can supply an adaptor for 110–120-volt, 60 Hz-appliances.

EMBASSIES AND CONSULATES

Australia: 6 Jalan Yap Kwan Seng; tel: 03-2146 5555; www. australia.org.my.
Canada: 17th Floor Menara Tan and Tan, 207 Jalan Tun Razak; tel: 03-2718 3333; www.malaysia.gc.ca.
Ireland: The Amp Walk, 218 Jalan Ampang; tel: 03-2161 2963; www.ireland-embassy.com.my.
New Zealand: 21st Floor Menara IMC, 8 Jalan Sultan Ismail; tel: 03-2078 2533; www.nzembassy.com. Visas are only issued in Singapore.
Singapore: 209 Jalan Tun Razak; tel: 03-2161 6277; www.mfa. gov.sg/kl.
Thailand: 206 Jalan Ampang; tel: 03-2148 8222; www.thaiembassy. org/kualalumpur.
UK: 185 Jalan Ampang; tel: 03-2170 2200; www.britain.org.my.
US: 376 Jalan Tun Razak; tel: 03-2168 5000; http://malaysia.us embassy.gov.

EMERGENCIES

Police/Ambulance/Fire Brigade: **999** (**112** from mobile phone)
Tourist Police: **03-2149 6590**

G

GAY AND LESBIAN TRAVELLERS

KL has perhaps Southeast Asia's most exciting gay scene, according to leading gay portal Utopia-Asia (www.utopia-asia.com/tipsmala.htm). The city has a large gay and lesbian community and a large variety of nightlife choices. KL-ites are generally tolerant – though not of public displays of affection – and appreciative of the pink dollar, so gay and lesbian visitors can travel safely and without fear of persecution in KL other than very occasional minor harassment from police. However, there are provisions in the Penal Code and, for Muslims, Islamic shariah laws, that penalise same-sex sexual acts and cross-dressing. For more information on the gay community, contact community rights and HIV/Aids outreach organisation, the PT Foundation (tel: 03-4044 4611; www.ptfmalaysia.org).

GETTING THERE

By air. Malaysia's national carrier is Malaysia Airlines (MAS; tel: 03-7843 3000, 1300-883 000 toll-free within Malaysia; www.malaysiaairlines.com), which flies between KL and over 100 domestic and international destinations, with direct flights from major cities. There are two local budget airlines: AirAsia (tel: 03-8775 4000; www.airasia.com), which flies to local and regional destinations including Australia; and Firefly (tel: 03-7845 4543; www.fireflyz.com.my), run by MAS, which has a Fokker 50 fleet covering northern Peninsular Malaysia and southern Thailand.

Thai Airways offers international flights via Bangkok and Singapore Airlines via Singapore. Besides these airlines, other airlines are worth considering. From North America: Air Canada, Cathay

Pacific, China Airlines, Emirates, EVA Air, Gulf Air and Qatar Airways (American Airlines fly to Singapore and Bangkok). Travel time from the west coast is 16 hours with a transit in Tokyo, Taipei or Hong Kong; from the east coast it is 22 hours via Europe.

From the UK: airlines include Air France, Air India, Alitalia, British Airways, Cathay Pacific, Emirates, EVA Air, Gulf Air, KLM and SriLankan Airlines. Travel time is 13 hours non-stop from Heathrow. From Australia, airlines include China Airlines, Emirates and Jetstar Airways. Travel time is eight hours from Sydney.

By rail. If you are in Bangkok or Singapore, you can take the train to the KL Sentral Station (Stesen Sentral KL). The KTMB (National Railways; tel: 03-2267 1200; www.ktmb.com.my) trains are modern, air-conditioned and efficient. Express services do not stop along the way except for the service from Bangkok, which requires a change of trains in Butterworth. Travel time is 20 hours from Bangkok and eight hours from Singapore.

By road. There are comfortable, air-conditioned express bus services from Bangkok and Singapore to KL. The main bus terminus in town is Puduraya (tel: 03-2070 0145) near Petaling Street. Buses from Bangkok terminate at Butterworth, where you change to a local bus, which then takes the excellent North–South Expressway to KL. Travel time is 21 hours. From Singapore, buses take six hours to reach KL; try to avoid crossing the very congested border checkpoints on Friday afternoons and during public holidays.

By sea. KL's closest seaport is Port Klang (Pelabuhan Klang), about 40km (25 miles) southwest, where ferries service Tanjung Balai, Sumatra, Indonesia (tel: 03-3167 1058); this is also the main port of call for regional cruise ships and international liners.

GUIDES AND TOURS

Hotels can generally arrange tours to any of the attractions listed in this book. To avoid scams, make sure tour agencies are registered with the Malaysian Association of Tour and Travel Agents, www.matta.org.my. Prices are usually around RM50–75 for half-day city tours and RM200–250 for full-day tours. Individual tour guides (Kuala Lumpur Tourist Guides Association, http://kltga.org.my) and car-and-driver outfits *(see page 110)* charge by the hour. For insurance purposes, make sure your service agents are licensed.

A great way to get to the main attractions is the **Kuala Lumpur Hop-on Hop-off Bus** (tel: 03-2691 1382; www.myhoponhopoff.com) which services 22 stops around the city. It runs every 30–45 minutes, from 8.30am–8.30pm, and you can get on and off the bus at any of the designated stops along the way. Pre-recorded commentary is available on board. Tickets (RM38) are valid for 24 hours and can be bought on the bus itself.

Recommended tour and travel agencies include: Asian Overland Services (tel: 03-4252 9100, www.asianoverland.com.my), Holiday Tours and Travel (tel: 03-2719 1800; www.holidaytours.com.my), Mayflower Acme Tours (tel: 03-6252 1888; www.mayflower.com.my), Diethelm Travel (tel: 03-2161 1922; www.diethelmtravel.com).

For nature and adventure tours, contact Asian Overland Services or Endemicguides.com (tel: 016-383 2222; www.endemicguides.com). For whitewater sports in Kuala Kubu Bahru, contact Tracks Adventures (tel: 019-344 3214, 03-6065 1767; www.tracksadventures.com.my), Pierose Swiftwater (tel: 013-361 3991, 03-6064 5040; www.raftmalaysia.com) or Khersonese Eco-X (tel: 016-690 2425, 03-7722 3511; www.thepaddlerz.com). For caving tours of the Dark Caves, Batu Caves, book with Green Heritage, tel: 012-310 3464.

H

HEALTH AND MEDICAL CARE

Malaysia has high health standards, ranking in the top 26 percent globally according to the World Health Organization's World Health Report 2007. It has experienced no major outbreaks of SARS or Avian Influenza (bird flu). However, prior to visiting the country, check the Malaysian Department of Public Health website (www. dph.gov.my) and get cholera, hepatitis A and B and tetanus shots. There are periodic outbreaks of dengue fever, for which there is no immunisation, so take preventive measures like using insect repellent, and if you suffer from a very high fever whilst or shortly after visiting Malaysia, consult a doctor immediately. Those with respiratory disorders should avoid visiting KL during the haze period.

While adjusting to the heat and humidity, hydrate yourself with at least 2 litres (8–10 glasses) of water a day and keep out of the sun between 11am–1pm. Drink boiled or bottled water or canned drinks. Avoid ice cubes in street-side stalls and small coffee shops, as the ice cubes here are usually made using unboiled water. Refrain from eating cut fruit from stalls.

KL has some of the best doctors in the region, who speak good English. Consultancy starts at RM30 for a GP and RM60 for a specialist. Private clinics abound, some open 24 hours a day, and pharmacies with licensed pharmacists are also plentiful. Major hotels have on-premises medical services. Government and private hospitals are well equipped and have specialised clinics, including **Hospital KL** (Jalan Pahang; tel: 03-2615 5555). Private hospitals include **Tung Shin Hospital** (Jalan Pudu, near Puduraya; tel: 03-2072 1655) and **Gleneagles Intan Medical Centre** (Jalan Ampang; tel: 03-4257 1300). Dental work is generally very good quality and reasonably priced. Dental clinics are located in major shopping malls.

doctor	**doctor**
hospital	**hospital**
clinic	**klinik**
medicine	**ubat**
I feel ill.	**Saya berasa sakit.**
I need a doctor.	**Saya perlu doctor.**
This is an emergency!	**Ini kecemasan!**

HOLIDAYS

Dates of cultural festivals vary as they are determined by lunar calendars. Check precise dates with Tourism Malaysia *(see page 126).*

New Year's Day	1 January
Federal Territory Day	1 February
Chinese New Year	January/February
Labour Day	1 May
Wesak Day	May
Agong's Birthday	First Sat in June
National Day	31 August
Deepavali	October/November
Christmas	December 25
Prophet Muhammad's Birthday	date varies
Hari Raya Puasa	date varies
Hari Raya Haji	date varies

L

LANGUAGE

The official language of Malaysia is Bahasa Malaysia or Malay. It is also known as Bahasa Melayu and popularly abbreviated as BM. Since it is the official language, all signboards and public displays of writing are in Bahasa Malaysia. However, it is an easy language to learn and is written in the roman alphabet. The language is polysyllabic, with variations in syllables to convey changes in meaning. Words are pronounced as they are spelt. You will find Sanskrit, Arabic, Tamil, Portuguese, Dutch and Chinese words in Bahasa Malaysia.

An increasingly large number of English words are being incorporated into the language, particularly terms related to business and information technology. At ground level, though, you are likely to encounter regional Malay dialects or a simplified form of Bahasa Malaysia known as *bahasa pasar* or 'bazaar Malay'.

Other languages that are widely used, mainly by the various ethnic groups, are Cantonese, Mandarin, Tamil and a colourful, localised form of English. When in doubt, revert to English and you might have more luck communicating.

1	satu	9	sembilan
2	dua	10	sepuluh
3	tiga	11	sebelas
4	empat	12	dua belas
5	lima	20	dua puluh
6	enam	21	dua puluh satu
7	tujuh	100	seratus
8	lapan	1,000	seribu

How do you do?	Apa khabar?
fine/good	baik
good morning	selamat pagi
good afternoon	selamat petang
good night	selamat malam
goodbye	selamat tinggal
bon voyage	selamat jalan
thank you	terima kasih
you're welcome	sama-sama
please	tolong/sila
excuse me	maafkan saya (maaf)
May I ask you a question?	Tumpang tanya?
I am sorry	minta maaf (maaf)
What is your name?	Siapa nama anda?
My name is…	Nama saya…
yes	ya
no	tidak (tak)

M

MAPS

Free, basic maps are available at most hotels and Tourist Information Centres. You can also purchase decent maps from any good bookshop or convenience stores; the *Insight Fleximap KL* is a good one to get.

MEDIA

The main English-language dailies are *The Star*, *The New Straits Times*, *The Sun* and the tabloid the *Malay Mail*. Most major hotels provide free local English-language newspapers every morning, or you can purchase them at any convenience store or bookshop. Business coverage is provided daily by *The Edge*. You can also buy *The Asian Wall Street Journal*, *The International Herald Tribune* and *USA Today*, as well as leading international periodicals and magazines at bookshops and hotel newsstands. Local lifestyle and entertainment magazines with news and listings include *Klue, Time Out*, *Vision KL* and *Faces*, which you can browse for free in cafés.

Popular English-language radio stations feature mainly American chart-toppers, with news hourly. FM stations include Hitz 92.9, Mix 94.5 and Light Radio 105.7. A flip through other stations will reveal an amazing spectrum of music, from canto-pop to Hindi movie hits.

Cable TV is available in most hotels, and usually includes CNN, BBC, CNBC and HBO. Free-to-air local TV stations are run by RTM (TV1 and TV2) and private stations TV3, NTV7, 8TV and 9TV. Except for TV1, which is a Malay-language station, all air local news reports in English, and mainstream American mini-series and comedies alongside religious Islamic programmes. Paid satellite TV station Astro has over 100 channels.

MONEY

Currency. Freely convertible, the Malaysian Ringgit (RM), also known as the dollar by the locals, is divided into 100 sen. Bank notes are denominated in units of 1, 2, 5, 10, 50 and 100. Coins are 5, 10, 20 and 50 sen (1 sen coins are being phased out).

Currency exchange. Banks and money changers are located everywhere in the city, including at the main bus and train terminals as well as at KLIA. Banks charge a commission whereas money-changers do not, but the latter's rates differ, so shop around for the best and try bargaining – larger amounts of currency get you better rates. Travellers' cheques are less readily accepted in KL except in banks.

Credit cards. American Express, Diners club, Visa and Mastercard are widely accepted at major shopping malls, hotels and petrol stations. Retailers add an extra 3 percent surcharge for the privilege of using plastic. As with everywhere in the world, be conscious of credit card fraud.

ATMs. ATMs are found in almost all bank branches, and particularly ones in the shopping malls. The operating hours for local machines are 6am–midnight, but some international banks operate 24 hours. You also can use your credit card to withdraw money from these machines. Banking networks available are MEPS, Cirrus, Maestro and BANKCARD.

OPENING TIMES

Businesses and government offices are on a five-day week, and follow an 8.30 or 9am to 5.30pm day. From Mon–Thur, most close for a one-hour lunch break beginning at 12.30 or 1pm. On Fri, the break is from 12.45–2.45pm to allow Muslims to perform prayers. Some businesses and government departments operate on Sat from 9am–1pm.

Banking hours are 9.30am–4pm Mon–Fri, although banks in shopping malls and areas like Masjid India, KLCC and Mid-Valley open from 10am–7pm weekdays and 10am–1pm on Sat. Money-changers are open until 7pm daily. Shops open six days a week between 9am and 11am and close between 9 and 11pm Mon–Sat, although some operate for a few hours on Sun. Shopping mall hours are 10am–10pm or 11am–11pm. There are 24-hour convenience stores all over the city.

Restaurants usually open from 11am–2.30pm and 5–11pm, while café hours are 7am–10pm. Eateries tend to close later at weekends, especially in tourist areas. *Mamak* outlets that serve Indian and Malay cuisines are open 24 hours a day, and some hawker centres are open for dinner and only close at 4am.

P

POST OFFICES

Although you take a bit of a chance with regular mail sent via the Malaysian postal service (www.pos.com.my), its registered mail, parcel and courier services (Poslaju) are good. You can also cash postal and money orders here. Post offices are found everywhere, and most are open Mon–Fri 8am–5.30pm and Sat 8am–1pm. The General Post Office (tel: 03-2274 1122; Mon–Sat 8am–6.30pm, Sun 10am–1pm) is located at Kompleks Dayabumi, beside Central Market. Post offices with extended hours from Mon–Sat are located in the Mid-Valley Megamall (9pm), Suria KLCC (6pm) and Sungai Wang Plaza (6pm). There is also a post office in KLIA (main building). Most big hotels can mail a letter for you.

International courier companies also operate in the city, including **FedEx** (The Weld Shopping Centre, Jalan Raja Chulan; tel: 1-800 88 6363) and **DHL** (Mail Boxes Etc., A-G-3A Ground Floor, Mid-Valley, near Boulevard Hotel; tel: 03-2282 7622).

PUBLIC TRANSPORT

Kuala Lumpur's public transport system is modern and efficient. Try to use the trains as much as possible to avoid vehicular traffic, which can be nightmarish during peak office hours (7.30–9.30am, 5–7pm) and when it rains. Be sure to carry enough small change for fares, especially when taking taxis.

Trains. Three train systems operate in KL and, with a bit of walking, these should get you to all the city's attractions. The Light Rail Transport (**LRT**; tel: 03-7625 6999; www.rapidkl.com.my) has two lines that intersect at Masjid Jamek and services the Golden Triangle, the old city centre, Kampung Baru and Petaling Jaya. The elevated **Monorail** (tel: 03-2273 1888) covers Petaling Street, Bukit Bintang, Kampung Baru, Brickfields and Titiwangsa. The **KTM Komuter** (tel: 03-2267 1200; www.ktmb.com.my) electrified commuter rail service has two lines that link downtown KL with the Klang Valley conurbation.

The central hub for all rail services is the ultra-modern KL Sentral Station (Stesen Sentral KL; tel: 03-2279 8888; www.stesensentral.com). Consider purchasing stored-value tickets for convenience.

Buses. Several companies provide bus services in KL, but the service is generally poor. Rapid KL (tel: 03-7625 6999; www.rapidkl.com.my) has the newest buses, and their City Buses (RM2 per day) cover downtown KL and link to many LRT stations. The main inner-city bus stops are Central Market/KL Sentral, Bukit Bintang, KLCC and Titiwangsa/Chow Kit. Buses are packed during peak periods, so watch your wallets. If you plan to cover all your chosen sights in 24 hours, the Kuala Lumpur Hop-on Hop-off Bus is a good option *(see page 116)*.

Taxis. Taxis are plentiful in KL, but drivers are getting a bad reputation for not using meters, which they are legally required to use, refusing to go to certain places and overcharging tourists. Check before you get into a taxi that they will use the meter and again that they do switch it on after you get in. If you are desperate, find out from your hotel concierge how much a ride should cost, and if you are prepared to pay a flat rate, make sure it is reasonable. Always be polite, and just walk away if the deal is not to your liking.

Taxis come in different colours, representing different companies, but all have a 'Teksi' sign on their roofs, which when lit signals availability. There are also premium taxis that have a RM4 flagfall and charge more per kilometre. Taxis can be hailed at taxi stands or flagged down in the street. KL Sentral and KL Tower have a coupon system which is more expensive, but could end up cheaper than bargaining with a recalcitrant driver. You can also telephone reliable taxi companies such as Comfort (tel: 03-8024 0507), Public Cab (tel: 03-6259 2020), Supercab (tel: 03-2095 3399) and Sunlight (tel: 03-9057 1111). Half- and full-day taxi charters to the Klang Valley cost RM20–25 per hour, excluding toll charges.

I would like to go to...	**Saya nak pergi ke...**
How much is the fare?	**Berapa harganya?**
Can I get small change?	**Boleh tukar duit kecil tak?**
Please use the meter.	**Sila guna meter.**

R

RELIGION

Mosques predominate to cater to KL's majority Muslim population, and all public buildings have at least a *surau* (prayer room). However, there are many place of worship for Buddhists, Taoists, Hindus, Sikhs and other belief systems.

Brickfields is home to churches of virtually all Christian denominations. The main Anglican church is the historic St Mary's Cathedral on Jalan Raja; the main Catholic church, the Cathedral of St John at 5 Jalan Bukit Nanas; and the main Methodist church is Wesley Methodist Church on 2 Jalan Wesley (near Puduraya).

T

TELEPHONES

The country code for Malaysia is '60' and the area code for KL and Selangor is '03', and Pahang, '09'. To call KL from overseas, dial

'603' followed by the number. For local and international telephone directory assistance, dial '103' (30 sen per call), and for operator assisted calls, '101' (70 sen per local call, RM2 per international call). To call overseas from KL, dial '00' followed by the country code, area code and phone number.

Most hotels offer International Direct Dial (IDD) services, but charges are high. Alternatively, some prepaid cards offer cheaper rates for international calls to certain destinations. These use Voice-Over-Internet-Protocol (VOIP), and the line might not be as clear. Ask the phone-card-sellers which cards give the best rates for the country you want to call.

There are public phones throughout the city operated either by coins – 10 sen per three minutes for a local call – or phone cards, available in denominations of RM5–50 from phone shops, news-stands and petrol stations. However, phone-booth vandalism is high, so it is worth bringing your mobile phone with you if you use the GSM band, as prepaid SIM cards are very affordable, starting at RM20 for registration and air time. The cards allow you to call locally and overseas, and cards and top-ups are widely available at phone shops as well as newsagents and petrol stations.

TIME ZONES

The standard Malaysian time is 8 hours ahead of GMT, 7 hours ahead of London, 12 hours ahead of New York and Toronto, and 3 hours behind Sydney. The country shares the same time zone with Singapore and Hong Kong.

TIPPING

Tipping is not obligatory, as bills usually include a 10 percent government tax and 5 percent service charge. However, tips are appreciated. Porters are usually tipped RM2–5, restaurant and bar staff are used to being left loose change or the rounding of the bill to the nearest denomination of 5 or 10, but obviously, you may tip according to how you feel about the quality of service. Otherwise, a simple thank-you *(terima kasih)* and a smile will do.

TOILETS

KL has a long way to go towards clean public toilets, although some of the ones in shopping malls have improved. Otherwise, expect dirty and wet toilets, and squat ones. Toilet paper is rare, although you can usually buy tissue paper at the toilet entrance. Most malls charge a toilet entrance fee of 20–50 sen. If you are very particular, pop into the nearest hotel and use their toilets.

Where is the toilet?	**Tandas di mana?**

TOURIST INFORMATION

Tourism Malaysia has a 24-hour infoline, 1300-88-5050 (within Malaysia only) and an excellent website, www.tourismmalaysia. gov.my. Tourist offices have helpful and trained staff, and ample information in the shape of brochures and maps.

Arrivals at the KLIA can visit the **Visitor Service Centre** at the Arrival Hall, Level 3, Main Building (tel: 03-8776 5651; 6am–midnight). The main information centre is at the **Malaysia Tourism Centre (MTC)** at 109 Jalan Ampang (tel: 03-9235 4848; daily 8am–10pm), which has officers, tourist literature and computers to surf state tourism homepages, a tour agency, the Transnasional interstate coach company, and a restaurant. Cultural performances are held on Tue, Thur, Sat and Sun, while theatre performances are staged sporadically in an auditorium. Tourist information is also available at **KL Sentral**, 2/F, Arrivals Hall, Kuala Lumpur City Air Terminal (tel: 03-2272 5823; daily 9am–6pm).

For a full list of Tourism Malaysia offices overseas, visit www. tourism.gov.my. Countries with offices include:

Australia: Level 2, 171 Clarence Street, Sydney, tel: 02-9299 4441.

Canada: 1590–1111, West Georgia Street, Vancouver, tel: 604-689 8899, 1-888 689 6872 (toll free).
UK: 57 Trafalgar Square, London, tel: 020 7930 7932.
US: 120 East 56th Street, Suite 810, New York, tel: 1 212 754 1113.

Related tourism organisations include **KL Tour Guide Association** (tel: 03-9221 0688; http://kltga.org.my), **Malaysian Association of Hotels** (tel: 03-4251 8477; www.hotels.org.my) and **Malaysian Association of Tour and Travel Agents** (tel: 03-9287 6881; www.matta.org.my).

W

WEBSITES AND INTERNET CAFÉS

Features and information on Kuala Lumpur and Malaysia can be found on All Malaysia **www.allmalaysia.info**, run by English newspaper, *The Star*, and travel portal Journeymalaysia **www.journeymalaysia.com**. For what's happening where in KL, Time Out Kuala Lumpur (**www.timeoutkl.com**) looks set to demolish all other listing sites, whereas arts aficionados will appreciate the no-holds-barred and spirited discourse in Kakiseni: **www.kakiseni.com**. Gourmands should check out Fried Chillies – **www.friedchillies.com** – which has food reviews galore. Nature-lovers should visit Wildasia – **www.wildasia.net**, which promotes responsible tourism and lists operators and activities. For alternative news on Malaysia, visit Aliran – **www.aliran.com**.

Internet cafés can be found in major shopping areas like Petaling Street and the KL City Centre, and rates start from RM2 per hour. However, a lot of internet cafés are for gaming and therefore filled with noisy youngsters. If you have your own computer, broadband internet is widely available, with wireless broadband (WiFi) available in KL's airports and increasingly offered for free in rooms of all budgets. WiFi is also free in cafés with a purchase of products; the cashier will provide you with the login name and password.

Recommended Hotels

Tourists have a good choice of international brands, home-grown chains, business hotels, themed resorts and boutique establishments, as well as serviced apartments, simple Chinese-run rest houses and backpacker hostels. Other than the budget accommodation, hotels are star-rated from 1 to 5 according to criteria such as size, facilities, number of staff and safety. For details, visit the Malaysian Association of Hotels website: www.hotels.org.my.

Below is a basic guide to the published rates for standard double rooms. Actual rates are usually lower, and internet rates among the best.

$$$$	over RM400
$$$	RM300–400
$$	RM100–300
$	under RM100

DATARAN MERDEKA

Heritage Station Hotel $ *Bangunan Stesen Keretapi, tel: 03-2273 5588, www.heritagehotelmalaysia.com.* A great location in the Old KL Railway Station, this once-grand hotel has downgraded to serve budget travellers, so even as you look out of the early 20th-century arched Mughal windows, the decor is contemporary and simple. Go for the larger family rooms.

Le Village $ *99A Jalan Tun H.S. Lee, tel: 013-355 0235.* Close to Medan Pasar Lama and Central Market, this homely and laid-back three-storey budget guesthouse has tiny rooms separated by partitions. The staff are friendly and there is a nice rooftop garden for chilling out. There is also complimentary use of the kitchen and free tea and coffee.

PETALING STREET

Hotel China Town (2) $ *70 and 72, Jalan Petaling, tel: 03-2072 9933, www.hotelchinatown2.com.* Simple and clean accommodation that is a mixture between a hotel and a hostel. Rooms are quiet, despite the fact the hotel is in the thick of Petaling Street. All rooms have air-conditioning and en suite bathrooms with hot showers, but only some have windows. Facilities include internet access, lockers, laundry and telephones.

Swiss-Inn Kuala Lumpur $$ *62 Jalan Sultan, tel: 03-2072 3333, www.swissgarden.com.* Converted from an early 20th-century shophouse, both the and front and back entrances of this popular inn open onto lively street action. Cast in pastel shades, rooms are basic and bathrooms small, but they are clean and good value for money. A non-smoking floor is available. Book online, as internet rates are much lower than published rates.

JALAN TUANKU ABDUL RAHMAN

Coliseum Café and Hotel $ *98–100 Jalan Tuanku Abdul Rahman, tel: 03-2692 6270.* Immerse yourself in the Old World charm of these rooms dating back to the 1920s. One of the first hotels in town, it housed less salubrious colonial characters who would drown their sorrows in the bar downstairs. Today, backpackers fill the 10 rooms – doubles are air-conditioned, singles are fan-cooled – and the view includes laundry drying on lines above the rooftops.

Tune Hotel $ *316 Jalan Tuanku Abdul Rahman, tel: 03-7962 5888, www.tunehotels.com.* This hotel uses the same formula as budget airlines (it is in fact linked to AirAsia): book online in advance or take advantage of special offers to get rates as low as RM9.99 a night. You do have to put up with advertisements that are used as decor, but in the almost bare rooms the specially designed beds assure guests of a good night's sleep, and the showers are luxurious.

LAKE GARDENS AND BRICKFIELDS

Boulevard Hotel $$ *Mid-Valley City, Lingkaran Syed Putra, tel: 03-2295 8000, www.blvhotel.com.* This 4-star business hotel is in Mid-Valley City, which has two enormous malls, so it is great for shopaholics, especially since the hotel is directly connected to one of the malls. The rooms are large, beautifully decorated and equipped with wireless internet. There is easy access to train stations.

Carcosa Seri Negara $$$$ *Persiaran Mahameru, Taman Tasik Perdana, tel: 03-2282 1888, www.ghmhotels.com.* This hotel offers a luxurious stay in beautifully restored colonial mansions with manicured gardens. In keeping with its past, the Carcosa continues to host dignitaries from around the world. Each suite is different, some coming with a terrace and others with separate dining, dressing and living rooms.

Hilton Kuala Lumpur $$$ *3 Jalan Stesen Sentral, tel: 03-2264 2264, www.hilton.co.uk/kualalumpur.* Soak up the style of this hip and happening Hilton with its luxurious beds, rainforest showers and huge plasma TVs. The rooms are bright, and floor-to-ceiling windows give great views of the city. There is also a fancy multi-restaurant enclave, and the Zeta Bar, which attracts a who's who of Kuala Lumpur.

Le Meridien $$$ *2 Jalan Stesen Sentral, tel: 03-2263 7888, www.le meridien.com.* Often unfairly overshadowed by the Hilton next door, this swanky establishment boasts ultra-contemporary decor, Jim Thompson upholstery and curtains, luxurious marble bathrooms, and a lovely resort-type free-form swimming pool area. Rooms and restaurants have great views of the city.

KLCC

Crowne Plaza Mutiara Kuala Lumpur $$$ *Jalan Sultan Ismail, tel: 03-2148 2322, www.crowneplaza.com.* Impeccable service is the hallmark of this hotel, which sports a fresh, contemporary look. Sitting in a beautifully landscaped 5-hectare (12-acre) property, its back entrance is five minutes from the Petronas Twin Towers. Executive club rooms and suites are luxuriously appointed.

Hotel Equatorial Kuala Lumpur $$$ *Jalan Sultan Ismail, tel: 03-2161 7777, www.equatorial.com/kul.* Pleasant, functional and comfortable, with amenities geared towards the business traveller. Its food and beverage outlets are among the city's most popular for corporate and personal dining. A shuttle goes daily to its pretty sister resort in Bangi, whose facilities can be used either with or without a room, for a day rate.

Hotel Imperial Kuala Lumpur $$$$ *Jalan Sultan Ismail, tel: 03-2717 9900, www.starwoodhotels.com.* Part of Starwood's 'luxury collection', this recently renovated hotel shows off plush Asian fittings such as Indian silks and Malay woodcarvings throughout the hotel. Conveniently located right next to the swish Asian Heritage Row.

Hotel Maya $$$ *138 Jalan Ampang, tel: 03-2711 8866, www.hotel maya.com.my.* Award-winning interior design and personalised service make this one of the best contemporary hotels in the area. Highlights of the rooms in this home-grown boutique resort hotel include rustic timber flooring and floor-to-ceiling glass panels overlooking either the Twin Towers or Kuala Lumpur Tower; the guests-only Sky Lounge provides views of both.

Impiana KLCC Hotel and Spa $$$ *13 Jalan Pinang, tel: 03-2147 1111, http://kualalumpurhotels.impiana.com.* Part of the Kuala Lumpur City Centre hotel cluster, this mid-range hotel sells itself as a spa retreat for commercial travellers. Its Swasana Spa has a wide choice of therapies and is located on the fourth floor, along with its infinity pool.

Mandarin Oriental Kuala Lumpur $$$$ *Kuala Lumpur City Centre, tel: 03-2380 8888, www.mandarinoriental.com.* Located in a prime position next to the Petronas Twin Towers, this super-luxury hotel has attentive service, large, well-appointed rooms with fabulous views of the Twin Towers, and a wide choice of good restaurants, with breakfasts often described as the best buffets in town. Guests also appreciate The Thalgo Marine Spa.

Pacific Regency Hotel Suites $$ *Menara PanGlobal, Jalan Punchak, off Jalan P. Ramlee, tel: 03-2332 7777, www.pacific-regency. com.* Those with children will appreciate the studios and two-bedroom family-style units, all with fully equipped kitchenettes and free wireless broadband access, in this hotel located opposite the

Kuala Lumpur Tower. Room service is available, and there is an in-house mini mart and delicatessen. The chic rooftop Luna Bar is one of the city's top hang-outs.

Renaissance Kuala Lumpur Hotel $$ *Corner of Jalan Sultan Ismail and Jalan Ampang, tel: 03-2162 2233, www.marriott.com.* Comprising two wings, the fancier European-themed Renaissance and the more modest New World, this hotel on the fringe of the Golden Triangle is popular with business travellers. The rooms are large but a little worn; the beds, however, are very comfortable, and the buffet breakfast and Olympic-sized swimming pool are real treats. The LRT and monorail are within walking distance.

Shangri-La Hotel Kuala Lumpur $$$$ *11 Jalan Sultan Ismail, tel: 03-2032 2388, www.shangri-la.com/kualalumpur.* Located just across the road from the pulsating clubs of Jalan P. Ramlee and close to the Kuala Lumpur Tower, this large hotel has comfortable, capacious rooms and lovely gardens. Popular among business folk, its foyer is always busy and the lounge often crowded. Likewise, its restaurants are good but popular at weekends, so bookings are essential.

Traders Hotel $$$ *Kuala Lumpur City Centre, tel: 03-2332 9888, www.shangri-la.com.* Connected to the Kuala Lumpur Convention Centre, this is a chic, contemporary hotel with garden rooms that offer spectacular views of the Petronas Twin Towers and KLCC Park. Catering to a mainly business clientele, it offers the same friendly treatment to tourists, too. The Sky Lounge has good night-time city views.

BUKIT BINTANG

Dorsett Regency Hotel Kuala Lumpur $$$ *172 Jalan Imbi, tel: 03-2715 1000, www.dorsettregency.com.my.* Set a little way from the Bukit Bintang buzz but close enough to the action, this 4-star facility boasts good service and value-for-money Esquire Club packages. Most rooms have a view of the Petronas Twin Towers. Health facilities and services range from chill baths to hot Jacuzzis and reflexology.

The Federal Kuala Lumpur $$$ *35 Jalan Bukit Bintang, tel: 03-2148 9166, www.federal.com.my.* Completed in 1957, just as Malaysia gained independence, this city landmark has kept up with the times and the competition. For one, it has an eco-floor boasting plastic-free, organic and eco-friendly products and services. Its fine-dining revolving restaurant offers panoramic city views. When you book, ask for a room with a view.

The Green Hut Lodge $ *48 Tengkat Tong Shin, tel: 03-2141 3339, www.thegreenhut.com.* Bright, spotless and safe, this stylish backpackers' lodge boasts ethnic interiors and bold colours, plus a well-designed common area. There is also a range of other backpacker facilities and services. Choose from twin and single rooms as well as dormitories; all rooms are air-conditioned and have hot showers.

Hotel Capitol Kuala Lumpur $$$$ *Jalan Bulan, Off Jalan Bukit Bintang, tel: 03-2143 7000, www.capitol.com.my.* While its lower-floor rooms can be noisy, this hotel's luxurious new '10 rooms' suites on the 19th and 20th floors are quiet and spacious, with 4m (13ft) high ceilings as standard and the largest suite measuring 56 sq m (602 sq ft). The modern decor includes comfortable sofas and lovely prints of KL, as well as floor-to-ceiling windows.

JW Marriott Kuala Lumpur $$$ *183 Jalan Bukit Bintang, tel: 03-2715 9000, www.marriott.com.* Designed for the business traveller, this hotel has all the requisite mod-cons, including separate work areas in the rooms. The hotel is part of the Starhill Gallery complex, so guests can use the mall's spa and health facilities as well as charging dining expenses at the 13 upscale restaurants in the basement Feast Village to their rooms. The hotel lobby can be very busy because it is linked to the mall, but Bukit Bintang and all that it offers is right on your doorstep.

Number Eight Guesthouse $ *8–10 Tengkat Tong Shin, tel: 03-2144 2050, www.numbereight.com.my.* A friendly, cosy concern showcasing Straits Chinese decor, this top-class budget guesthouse has twins, doubles and dormitories in its Budget wing and en suites in its Boutique wing. Facilities and services include air conditioning/

fans, hot showers, a spacious lounge area, free 24-hour internet access (including WiFi) and a big DVD collection.

Red Palm $ *5 Tengkat Tong Shin, Bukit Bintang, tel: 03-2143 1279, www.redpalm-kl.com.* Located along the backpackers' row, this award-winning hostel scores points for its warm family atmosphere. All backpacker facilities are available, including copious tourist information. Dorms and rooms available.

The Ritz-Carlton Kuala Lumpur $$$$ *168 Jalan Imbi, tel: 03-2142 8000, www.ritzcarlton.com.* Linked to Starhill Gallery, this luxury boutique hotel's personalised butler service is its trademark. With an area of 45 sq m (484 sq ft) and 3m (9ft) high ceilings, the guest rooms are also among KL's largest hotel rooms. Indulge in outdoor spa baths and a wide range of therapies at its beautiful tropical Spa Village.

The Westin Kuala Lumpur $$$$ *199 Jalan Bukit Bintang, tel: 03-2731 8333, www.westin.com/kualalumpur.* Located at the end of the Bintang Walk strip, next to Starhill Gallery and opposite The Pavilion shopping mall, this contemporary 5-star hotel boasts superbly comfortable beds, a good Kids' Club and babysitting services, as well as the popular Latin venue, Qba.

OUTSIDE KUALA LUMPUR

Genting Highlands Resort $$–$$$$ *tel: 03-2718 1118, www.genting.com.my/en/accommodation.* Choose from the 5-star Genting Hotel and Highlands Hotel (where the casino is), the 4-star Resort Hotel, or the 3-star Theme Park Hotel (where the indoor theme park sits) and First World Hotel (the world's largest hotel). Rooms at the lower star-rated hotels are small and peak-period check-ins excruciatingly slow. The Awana Genting Highlands Golf and Country Resort, midway up, is less hectic and is set in lovely green surroundings.

Highland Resthouse Holdings (HRH) Bungalows, Fraser's Hill $$–$$$$ *Suite 38A-1, 38th Floor, Empire Tower, City Square Centre, 182 Jalan Tun Razak, tel: 03-2164 8937, www.hrhbungalows.com.* Scattered throughout the highlands, these beautifully renovated colonial bungalows provide contemporary comfort. Complete with dining and living rooms, most of the bungalows are only available for rent whole, except for Pekan Bungalow, whose eight rooms can be rented individually. Meals can be arranged. Do not confuse these bungalows with the government-run FHDC bungalows, which are older.

Hilton Petaling Jaya $$ *2 Jalan Barat, Petaling Jaya, tel: 03-7955 9122, www.hilton.com.* Primarily a business hotel, this Hilton is a little worn – ask for rooms in the new wing – but clean and conveniently located in Petaling Jaya close to public transport to KL and lots of local shops and eateries. Don't miss the outstanding Malaysian spread at its popular restaurant, Paya Serai.

Kuala Selangor Nature Park $ *Jalan Klinik, tel: 03-3289 2294, email: ksnaturepark@yahoo.com.* Staying at the park is the best way to hear dawn bird choruses and gorgeous moonlit sonatas, as well as catch sight of otters and monkeys. Accommodation is basic, and you need to bring your own towels and toiletries, but there is running water and 24-hour electricity, as well as a common kitchen (usage fee applies for non-chalet guests). Come well prepared for mosquitoes. For meals, walk 10 minutes to the old town centre.

The Smokehouse Hotel and Restaurant, Fraser's Hill $$ *Jalan Jeriau, tel: 09-362 2226, www.thesmokehouse.com.my/fh.htm.* This former Red Cross building boasts beautiful stone masonry, well-manicured English gardens and sumptuous Devonshire cream teas. Rooms are cosy and every one is different, offering a choice of hill or garden views. Common areas are filled with chintz and memorabilia. A fire is lit every evening, and guests are required to dress for dinner.

Sunway Resort Hotel and Spa $$$$ *Persiaran Lagoon, tel: 03-7492 8000, www.sunway.com.my/hotel.* A Malaysian version of South Africa's Palace of the Lost City, this is a hit with families as it is just a short walk away from the Sunway Lagoon theme park and Pyramid shopping centre. It has a great landscaped swimming pool and an excellent Italian restaurant. Part of the hotel is underground; avoid rooms just beneath the lobby, as it can be noisy overhead.

Recommended Restaurants

With eating out being Malaysians' favourite pastime, the range of food and eateries is breathtaking. From regional specialities dished up at roadside stalls to molecular gastronomy in fine-dining restaurants, visitors would be hard-pressed to resist Kuala Lumpur's culinary charms. What's more, food is available around the clock. Beer is served in most non-Muslim eateries, and wine is increasingly available in the fancier restaurants.

The price symbols below are intended as a guide, and are based on a standard meal for two without drinks.

$$$$	over RM90
$$$	RM60–90
$$	RM30–60
$	under RM30

DATARAN MERDEKA

Ginger Restaurant $$ *Lot M12 Central Market, Jalan Hang Kasturi, tel: 03-2273 7371.* Open daily 11am–10pm. Gorgeous Thai, Indonesian and Malay artefacts reflect this cosy eatery's menu. Must-tries here are the spicy Malay *rendang* (dry beef or chicken curry), Thai green chicken curry and Indonesian fried rice accompanied by satay.

Precious Old China Restaurant and Bar $$ *Lot 2, Mezzanine floor, Central Market, tel: 03-2273 7372.* Open daily 11.30am–9.30pm. Vietnamese deities, Victorian furniture and Chinese antique wall panels decorate this Nyonya restaurant. Traditional recipes are superbly executed, with complex spices infusing the meats, and the curries are nicely rich. Do not miss dessert.

Sin Seng Nam Restaurant $ *2 Medan Pasar, tel: 03-2078 5359.* Open Monday–Friday 7am–2.30pm. This old Hainanese coffee shop in the oldest part of Yap Ah Loy's Chinatown keeps its original fittings and menus. Try its delicious Hainanese chicken rice, curry chicken or stir-fried noodles. Traditional breakfast of toast with *kaya* (coconut jam), half-boiled egg and coffee is also served.

PETALING STREET

Chinatown Seng Kee $ *50 Jalan Sultan, tel: 03-2072 5950*. Open daily 11am–4.30pm. This chirpy eatery is a great place to eat excellent Chinese-style noodles. Try the KL speciality, Hokkien *mee* (fat, yellow egg noodles stir-fried in dark soy) or the eatery's signature claypot *loh shu fun* (rice noodles in a minced-pork sauce).

Hong Ngek Restaurant $ *50 Jalan Tun H.S. Lee, tel: 03-2078 7852*. Open Monday–Saturday 10am–7pm. An old Chinese restaurant dating back to the 1940s, with air-conditioning upstairs. Hokkien-style Chinese food is served here, a speciality being pomfret cooked in two styles: deep-fried and steamed. The Hokkien *mee* is excellent and it is also worth trying the oyster omelette.

Nam Heong $ *56 Jalan Sultan, tel: 03-2078 5879*. Open daily 10am–3pm. With a 50-year reputation for traditional Hainanese chicken rice, this eatery can be packed and the chicken sold out by 1pm. Luckily, their barbecued pork *(char siu)* and roast pork are excellent, too. Have your choice of meat with beautifully fragrant rice cooked in chicken stock, accompanied by ginger, garlic and chilli.

Peter Hoe Beyond $ *2nd floor Lee Rubber Building, 145 Jalan Tun H.S. Lee, tel: 03-2026 9788*. Open daily 10am–7pm. Simple, wholesome fare is the order of the day at this tiny, chic café located within a terrific boutique. Munch on quiches, pies and salads, or, if it is teatime, scones and cakes.

Soong Kee Beef Noodles $ *3 Jalan Silang, tel: 03-2078 1484*. Open Monday–Saturday 11am–midnight, closed public holidays. This simple eatery with just a handful of tables and chairs has been making the best beef dumplings in the city for over six decades. Enjoy them in a soup accompanied by fine springy egg noodles in a dark sauce with minced beef and garlic.

JALAN MASJID INDIA AND JALAN TAR

Coliseum Café $ *98–100 Jalan Tuanku Abdul Rahman, tel: 03-2692 6270.* Open daily 10am–10pm. Get whisked back to the British colonial days in this café. Guzzle down a gunner (a mix of ginger ale, ginger beer and bitters), then embark on a sizzling rib-eye steak or a baked crabmeat salad and fried prawn fritters with tartare sauce. The English pot pies here are still baked in a firewood oven.

Sagar Café $ *Ground Floor, Semua House, Lorong Bunus 6.* Open daily 8am–8pm. This café is the affordable and accessible branch of one of the city's oldest names in fine North Indian cuisine. Its self-service, alfresco approach keeps prices low, and its location lets diners enjoy the bustle of Jalan Masjid India while partaking in its famous *naan*, chicken and *dhal* preparations.

Saravanaa Bhavan $ *1007 Selangor Mansion, Jalan Masjid India, tel: 03-2287 1228.* Open daily 8.30am–11pm. Delicious Indian vegetarian food is served in this pretty chain restaurant. An extensive menu offers everything from breads to rice, and even Chinese Indian preparations. The set meals are good value and the sweets are delectable and good with *masala* tea or Bru coffee.

KAMPUNG BARU

Gerai 21 $ *Pintu Gerbang, Jalan Raja Muda Musa, tel: 019-306 2753.* Open daily 10am–2am. With colourful fairy lights and a large, airy open area, this casual eatery is particularly good at night. Pick a dish from the numerous food stalls. Recommended are the *ikan bakar*, charcoal-grilled fish and *nasi lauk*, where you choose from over 20 Malay dishes to accompany your steamed rice.

Nasi Lemak Mak Wanjor $ *8 Jalan Raja Muda Musa.* Open daily 7am–noon, Monday–Saturday 4pm–1am. Queue up for one of KL's best preparations of Malaysia's favourite breakfast, *nasi lemak*. Have your fluffy, steamed rice with a simple, sweetish anchovy *sambal* (chilli paste) and hard-boiled egg, or add squid, beef *rendang* or curry chicken. Wash it down with a hot local tea or coffee.

Pasar Minggu $ *Jalan Raja Muda Musa.* Open daily 7am–noon. A no-frills hawker centre where stall number GSA14 serves delicious Javanese *lontong,* a soupy compressed-rice and vegetable dish where the rice roll is uniquely steamed in a banana leaf, and GSA13 serves the hard-to-find *kuih lopis,* a triangular glutinous rice dessert coated in desiccated coconut and served with palm sugar.

Wong Solo $ *57 Jalan Raja Alang, tel: 03-2691 1680.* Open daily 11.45am–11pm. This franchise of a popular Indonesian chain is famous for its tasty, tender meats, available in handy set meals. A quirky offering – though feminists might not be amused – is Jus Poligami (Polygamy Juice), a four-fruit juice mix honouring the owner's four wives. The outlet is impeccably clean; there is a small section where you can sit on the floor and dine at a low table *(lesehan).*

LAKE GARDENS AND BRICKFIELDS

The Gulai House, Carcosa Seri Negara $$$$ *Persiaran Mahameru, tel: 03-2295 0888.* Open daily noon–3pm, 7–10.30pm. This elegant Malay fine-dining restaurant is located in the beautiful colonial former home of the British Governor-General. The menu includes traditional Malay favourites as well as a selection of North Indian dishes. Book ahead for the popular Sunday curry tiffin lunch (noon–3pm). Note that there is a dress code.

Museum Restaurant and Café $$$ *Islamic Arts Museum Malaysia, Jalan Lembah Perdana, Kuala Lumpur, tel: 03-2274 2020.* Open Tuesday–Sunday 10am–6pm. Dine in sumptuous surroundings with lacy wall carvings and mirror-work pillars, the work of Moroccan craftsmen. Glass walls overlook a fountain garden. Enjoy excellent Middle Eastern dishes, leaving room for the exquisite baklava.

Sri Paandi $ *254 Jalan Tun Sambanthan, Brickfields, tel: 03-2274 0464.* Open 24 hours. This no-frills eatery serves typical Tamil banana-leaf meals comprising steamed rice and a choice of curries such as chicken *varuval* and mutton curry, or *tenggiri* (mackerel) deep-fried on the spot. Wash your meal down with an iced *lassi* yoghurt drink or piping hot *teh tarik* ('pulled' tea).

Vischalachirs $ *19 Jalan Travers, Brickfields, tel: 03-2274 6819.* Open daily 11am–10.45pm. This simple Chettiar family-run restaurant serves excellent traditional meals that are subtle blends of sweet, sour and lightly spicy. A typical set is rice with *sambar* (stew made from pulses) and *puli kulambu* (tamarind curry); end with sweet *payasam* (pudding).

KLCC

Aseana Café $ *Lot G11-20, G/F, Suria KLCC, tel: 03-2382 0395.* Open daily 10am–10pm. Dine amidst the Aseana Gallery's beautiful Asian furnishings and bric-a-brac, all of which are for sale. Outdoor seating is also available. Decadent Malay snacks are on offer, as well as heartier meals such as *nasi campur,* a rice dish served with five accompaniments.

CoChine Lounge and Restaurant $$$$ *64 Jalan Doraisamy, Asian Heritage Row, tel: 03-2697 1180.* Open Monday–Saturday noon–midnight. This restaurant has sumptuously luxurious decor, complete with Buddhist sculptures and carvings, and water features amid lush foliage. Have a cocktail at the bar downstairs before heading upstairs to the fine-dining restaurant, where you can sink into plush chairs and savour food from Cambodia, Vietnam and Laos.

Hakka Restaurant $$ *6 Jalan Kia Peng, tel: 03-2143 1908.* Open daily noon–3pm, 6pm–midnight. A large Chinese restaurant with an open courtyard that is great for night dining and good value for money to boot, this is *the* place to come to for authentic Hakka food. In general, Hakka cuisine is salty, fragrant and fatty, and features a wide range of pickled food and rich, textured sauces. Signature dishes include beggar's chicken (baked salted chicken) and *mui choy kau yoke* (braised pork belly layered with preserved vegetables).

Palacio $$$$ *Jalan Doraisamy, Asian Heritage Row, tel: 03-2692 0992.* Open daily 6–11pm. Have your fill of tasty tapas at this Franco-Spanish outfit's funky tapas bar, which is equipped with soft velvet cushions and retro chairs. Upstairs, in the contemporary restaurant, exquisitely prepared meals come beautifully displayed on your plate and in generous portions to boot. The must-tries here are the 'Trios', French specialities cooked in three different styles.

Restaurant Lafite $$$$ *Shangri-la Hotel, 11 Jalan Sultan Ismail, tel: 03-2074 3900*. Open Monday–Friday noon–2.30pm, Monday–Saturday 7 10.30pm. The current 'in' place for molecular gastronomy; award-winning chef Kevin Cherkas, formerly of Spain's stunningly innovative El Bulli, has revolutionised Lafite's menu using new food preparation methods and technology. Expect quirky combinations of flavours and textures such as liquids that burst from congealed membranes, and light-as-air mushroom foam toppings.

Still Waters $$$ *Hotel Maya Kuala Lumpur, 138 Jalan Ampang, tel: 03-2711 8866*. Open daily noon–2.30pm, 6.30–10.30pm. Stylish, serene ambience with water features all around sets the mood for *'sosaku'* or creative Japanese cuisine. The balance of fresh Japanese ingredients and cooking styles from all over the world yields unorthodox and interesting results. Not your typical sushi bar.

Yut Kee $ *35 Jalan Dang Wangi, tel: 03-2698 8108*. Open Tuesday–Sunday 7am–6pm. A popular, atmospheric Hainanese coffee shop dating back to the 1920s, well known for *roti babi*, a sandwich filled with minced pork and crabmeat, dipped in egg and deep-fried and served with Worcestershire sauce. Another must-try is the Swiss roll with *kaya* (coconut jam). An assortment of noodles is also available.

BUKIT BINTANG

Enak $$$ *LG2 Feast Floor, Starhill Gallery, 181 Jalan Bukit Bintang, tel: 03-2141 8973*. Open daily noon–midnight. Step into an elegant interior with brass antiques and sculptures. Creative takes on traditional Achenese and Malay cuisine, beautifully presented. Calorie-counters should note that there is liberal use of coconut milk and deep-frying, but the food is delicious.

Food Republic $ *Lower Ground, Pavilion Kuala Lumpur, Jalan Bukit Bintang, tel: 03-2142 8006*. Open daily 10am–10pm. An upmarket food court featuring local and regional eats. Its 28 outlets include street food such as Thye Hong's *char kway teow* quirkily served in tree bark, and snacks such as John King's durian tart, a Hong Kong egg tart that features the king of Malaysian fruits.

J. CO Donuts and Coffee $ *Lot 1.05.00, First Floor, Pavilion Kuala Lumpur, Jalan Bukit Bintang, tel: 03-2141 7761*. Open daily 10am–10pm. Queues signal the cult-like status of this Indonesian outlet which churns out doughnuts by the dozen. It is hard to resist the soft, spongy dough and dazzling array of toppings.

Kedai Ayam Panggang Wong Ah Wah $ *1, 3, 5, 7 and 9 Jalan Alor, off Jalan Bukit Bintang, tel: 03-2148 3413*. Open daily 5pm–3.45am; closed one Monday a fortnight. One of the best-known restaurants along this bustling food street. Fried chicken wings are the main draw, but there is a huge selection of Cantonese dishes to pick from, too. Dine alfresco or in air-conditioned comfort.

Passage Through India $$ *4 Jalan Delima, off Bukit Bintang, tel: 03-2145 0366*. Open daily noon–2.30pm, 6.30–11pm. Housed in an old bungalow, this restaurant scores for atmosphere and a massive menu that lives up to its name by offering a range of Indian delights from Goan seafood to meats from Assam. Try the *dum biryani* (a special preparation of rice and spiced meat), the divine fish tikka and the excellent prawn *jalfrazi*.

Restoran Kam Fatt $ *37 Jalan Changkat Tong Shin, tel: 03-2148 3105*. Open daily 6am–2.30pm. Pop in for a Chinese coffee-shop breakfast. Enjoy well-toasted bread spread with butter and *kaya* (coconut jam) with your tea or coffee. Alternatively, select from an assortment of noodles, rice porridge, Chinese cakes and dumplings.

Restoran Tarbush $$ *138 Jalan Bukit Bintang, tel: 03-2142 8558*. Open daily 10am–1am. A leather camel stands guard over the lush interior lit by filigree lamps. It's all a far cry from this restaurant's humble beginnings in 1988 as a sandwich bar. Tarbush stays true to the heart of Lebanese cuisine: liberal use of fresh vegetables, copious amounts of garlic and olive oil and well-marinated grilled meats. This restaurant also has outlets in Suria KLCC and Starhill.

INDEX

Berlitz pocket guide

Kuala Lumpur

First Edition 2008

Written by Siew Lyn Wong
Edited by Anna Tyler
Series Editor: Tony Halliday

Photography credits
Getty Images 20; Ingo Jezierski 31; Private Archives 15, 16, 18, 19; Jon Santa Cruz 3(tr), 6, 8, 11, 12, 22, 28, 35, 44, 55, 56, 57, 66, 69, 73, 78, 87, 89, 102; Tourism Malaysia 99; Nikt Wong 3(c), 17, 24, 26, 29, 32, 33, 36, 37, 38, 40, 41, 43, 45, 47, 48, 49, 51, 52, 54, 58, 60, 61, 63, 65, 71, 72, 74, 75, 77, 79, 80, 81, 82, 84, 88, 90, 92, 94, 97, 100, 101, 104.

Cover picture: Anthony Brown/Alamy

All Rights Reserved
© 2008 Berlitz Publishing/Apa Publications GmbH & Co. Verlag KG, Singapore Branch, Singapore

Printed in Singapore by Insight Print Services (Pte) Ltd, 38 Joo Koon Road, Singapore 628990. Tel: (65) 6865-1600. Fax: (65) 6861-6438

Berlitz Trademark Reg. U.S. Patent Office and other countries. Marca Registrada

Every effort has been made to provide accurate information in this publication, but changes are inevitable. The publisher cannot be responsible for any resulting loss, inconvenience or injury.

Contact us

At Berlitz we strive to keep our guides as accurate and up to date as possible, but if you find anything that has changed, or if you have any suggestions on ways to improve this guide, then we would be delighted to hear from you.

Berlitz Publishing, PO Box 7910,
London SE1 1WE, England.
fax: (44) 20 7403 0290
email: berlitz@apaguide.co.uk
www.berlitzpublishing.com